To Nick

With all best wishes and many happy memories.

FACING THE WIND

FACING THE WIND

BOB LAMB

Gunner Enterprises

First published in 2020 by Gunner Enterprises

ISBN 978-1-8382488-0-2

Copyright © Bob Lamb, 2020

Edited by Sarah Walker

The right of Bob Lamb to be identified as the author of this work has been asserted in accordance with the Copyright, Designs and Patents Act, 1988.

All rights reserved. No part of this publication may be reproduced, stored in a retrieval system, or transmitted, in any form or by any means (electronic, mechanical, photocopying, recording or otherwise), without the prior written permission of the publisher.

A CIP catalogue record for this book is available from the British Library.

Printed and bound by IngramSpark.

Typesetting & cover design by Sarah Walker via IngramSpark

Vicki, James, Chris & Bob Lamb

This book would never have become words without the inspiration of my wonderful family, Christina, Vicki and Jim. Their joy of life and belief that we can always overcome if we want to enough, sustained me in those early hours.

I must also thank all the friends and visitors whose stories, wit and humour enriched my life. I know I have been a very lucky man in very many ways and acknowledge the parts played by so many.

The family home & lake at Manor Farm

I

CHAPTER ONE

I woke to the monotonous drumming of snow on the old slate roof and the warming feeling that followed. A symbolic duvet to keep out the chill of the world. The clock by the bed showed four twenty-seven. Why did I always wake at four twenty-seven these days? If only I could be as consistent during the useful daylight hours, I might not have so much to worry about when I did wake at four twenty-seven. In these early hours, all thoughts seem to cycle in ever-tightening circles, rarely leading to anything positive and often leaving me with an inner sense of uselessness - and a need to go to the loo, before bringing forward the onset of the new day by lighting the fire and making a cup of tea.

I had reached the tea-brewing stage and all was running to form, when I suddenly had an idea. I suppose it was not so much an idea, as the coming together of several facts and thoughts that had been pointlessly floating around inside my head with no particular place to go.

Fact one: our son, who had been diagnosed with dyslexia, had suddenly lost his extra help at the local school thanks to the arrival of a new headmistress, who had the unfortunate notion that dyslexia was something you should just snap out of.

Fact two: the only remedy seemed to be a private school, evidenced by the prospectuses spread haphazardly on the dresser nearby. Rather like a pile of glossy holiday brochures, they drew you in, only to hit you with the price list and compulsory 'optional' extras.

Our farm was small, less than two hundred acres, and dry. Even an optimistic land agent would struggle to call it 'prime'. The buildings had been superb at the turn of the century but were now crying out for new roofs and easier access. All this at a time of rapidly falling prices and disappearing subsidies. The thought of private schools could not have come at a worse time.

At this stage, my subconscious mental survival package set in. 'Now then, there must be some good in all this', my brain muttered. 'What about the beauty of the farm, the wonderful old farmhouse, the joy it gives you having guests - how about injecting these into your equation?'

And so, with the teapot still brewing on the cold February morning, the idea of Bed and Breakfast hatched in my mind. My wife, Chris, will doubtless point out that she had been considering this option for some time, had drawn many diagrams and costings to prove the point to herself and that, as the work would fall mostly to her, the idea was not mine to have. This apart, I returned to bed with a significantly brighter step than the one that had carried me precariously down the stairs two hours earlier. I glanced out of the landing window; the snow was still falling, but the drumming had gone and felt more like a pat on the head.

Night-borne ideas follow one of two routes. The first is when they crop up at breakfast next morning with flowing enthusiasm and rampant arguments that will put the world to rights at a stroke, but then dissolve as the sun mounts the yardarm. Their charm vanishes with the beauty of the haw frost and I quietly leave the house to check the sheep, firmly telling myself that I will never have a nocturnal idea again.

The other route is when I sleep so soundly when I do return to bed, that I wake so late and so tired that I forget the idea completely until I stop for a cup of coffee, or wait for the old, lame ewe to make up the hundred-yard gap that has developed between the rest of the flock and herself as they move slowly from one field to another. This is the route for real ideas. The ewe has passed me by now, the gate post is giving support and my mind is checking the credentials of the night-time working. By the time I have agreed, and cross-checked that I still like the idea, the sheep will be two fields away and busily enjoying my neighbour's wheat crop.

It was lunchtime before I mentioned the idea to Chris. Her wry smile was followed by the production of a diary full of costings and figures, room decorations and furnishings. Faded green, and with as many poorly fitting additions as original pages, she opened it with as much glee as a clergyman would open a bible before a sinner.

'These early pages are the work we have already done - the sitting room and the kitchen - you like those, don't you?' She was moving at great speed, carried by her enthusiasm. I felt lost and lead footed.

'Yes', I replied, with disbelief in my throat.

'If we decorate these bedrooms...', she continued, pointing at her masterplan which had magically unfolded, well-thumbed and with its many additions marked in many different pens, 'and change the bathroom like this...', again another page, another plan, 'we will greatly improve the house and be able to take guests. What do you think?'

I had thought our previous ideas to have been spontaneous discussions, openly carried out, decisions compromisingly made. Now I saw I had merely agreed to the plans she had already conceived, planted in my mind, and allowed to hatch as supposedly common thoughts. I had to smile.

'Yes dear, they are beautiful and so are you.' I gave her a kiss on the cheek and turned to more mundane tasks. A man can only take so much outflanking.

The seed was sown that chilly morning. The pile of school prospectuses lost their menace and, with a renewed belief in life, we looked through them again. The closer I looked, the more like holiday brochures they appeared; but now it was more like choosing a holiday we had decided to take instead of festive window shopping.

'The Independent Schools advisory service has sent us these, based on locality and dyslexia facilities.' Chris shuffled half a dozen booklets in front of me. She didn't say 'pick a card' or 'close your eyes and stab a pin', but I felt just as qualified. I selected the one nearest me and read it; in turn we glanced through them without speaking. After several minutes we looked at each other before simultaneously pointing at the same booklet.

'I'll arrange a visit for next week,' said Chris, getting up and carrying our half-full teacups with her. Yes, I thought, next week before I'm too busy. I smiled to myself, thinking,

'You liar, you mean next week before you run out of courage... before you think of the consequences.'

It was now decided that we would do Bed and Breakfast and that the money would pay for James's school fees. That the latter would be expensive and the former totally unknown didn't matter, it had been decided, the commitment made. It would work!

Our farm stretches like a bent thumb upstream from the village. Since my father's retirement and the decision to dissolve the partnership with my brother, our farming has been based on a pedigree sheep flock and small area of barley. In those far-off halcyon days when prices rose every year and dreams of selling every sheep for vast sums seemed there for the taking, the fact that my standing as a farmer was dubious did not cross my mind. In late school years when everyone is expected to have fine ambitions, mine was to retire or, if necessary, to be a journalist.

I recall the essay entitled 'What I hope to achieve by the time I'm forty' and the teacher's deep gloom at my wish to have finished my working life by then. It took hours to convince him that this was real ambition, that however much you liked a job there would be bits you would hate. Only when you are retired, self-sufficient and free of work demands can you do just what you want, when you want. He was never really convinced. My subconscious desire to skirt around the practical aspects of life, which manifest themselves as broken-down machinery and leaking water pipes, has always been a pain, but one which a prosperous economy had let me forget. So, as the prospects of lower prices conflicted with our new educational need it was time to take stock.

I have never been a believer in acknowledging my weaknesses, it smells too much of negative thinking. Far better to search for any strengths and lean on them till it hurts. I had a great-grandfather noted for his ability not only to sleep through any church sermon, but also to talk for any amount of time without actually saying anything. My mother has often likened me to him and, although we never met, I feel a certain affinity with him. At thirty-six, I had to admit that retirement by forty was highly unlikely. It became increasingly obvious that the only way forward for me, the farm and eternity, was to become people orientated. Simplify the farm to make full use of our specialist sheep flock, and thereafter concentrate on the subject that had held me in good stead at school and college, and at which I still felt most at home; namely, waffle!

Bed and Breakfast is about people. Too obvious, perhaps, but anyone embarking on it without a natural liking for people may as well stay in bed, roll over, and wait for another nocturnal idea to strike. We had always liked a house full of guests, something we had inherited from our farming families. Whether it was the ever-changing array of faces and characters, or something as simple as giving people a good time, we didn't need to know. But, as we prepared ourselves for our first guests, we carried with us this pride in our home that would soon be shared with others - at a price.

Winter is not a time when you are rushed off your feet with potential guests hammering at the door. It is a time for preparing for the rush that will come with the spring bulbs, fluffy lambs and white fleecy clouds, as people feel the need to escape their urban environment or take holidays in the Old Country. This is the point where, in a well-ordered world, I could report on our beaver-like efforts to prepare ourselves for this mad influx of guests. We didn't. Well, we made sure the bedrooms were decent and the bathroom had an overhaul, but there was no beavering. The latent fear of turning our home into a mini hotel, the ease of not doing much and the confidence that our personas would carry us through prevailed. We would feel our way, see if we liked it. There was no rush.

One of our first purchases was a Visitors' Book. Whether as literal evidence of our intentions or merely out of bravado, a poor joke, it found its way into the house along with a few cans of paint. Many years before I had given my mother a similar book. Along with the ongoing visitors that a farming family with a large farmhouse can expect, my brother and I had reached the age when our boarding school friends wanted to flock to the country. Some came many times, some, having slept in our totally unheated bedrooms in February or pitched their tent next to the chicken run on a summer's morning, found other challenges that they could face. Either way, their comments in the visitors' book became not just a record; wit and originality became as important as absolute accuracy. A polite, to the point remark after a first visit became bolder by the third and positively sharp by the fifth.

Mother took them all with the same grace; her love of people and especially children was universal. 'Bedroom cold but warmer than bathroom' was one famous entry by a frequent visitor.

Summer holidays were most popular, both with friends helping bring in the harvest, and those who just came to heckle.

'Five-star rating not applicable due to the gluttony of the semi-permanent staff' was one view of a bale slinger's appetite. I could picture our school friend Rusty at the old Formica-topped kitchen table. He could eat a loaf of bread at a sitting, chaff gently falling from his overgrown hair onto whatever spread he had chosen. Everything was done by hand in those days, bales stacked and sacks wheeled. Days seemed to last for ever in a haze of humour and energy before dissolving into total exhaustion.

'How much do you want for this lot of barley?', the corn merchant would say, catching a double handful of grain as it flowed from the cleaner into the sack.

'£25 a quarter', my father would say, quoting those old imperial measures that seemed to roll off the tongue like poetry. A quarter was a measurement of volume rather than weight and was not actually a quarter of anything that I discovered. There were five quarters to a ton of barley. 'I think it's worth more than that', the merchant would reply with a smile that said he thought the opposite.

'Let's discuss it in the office.'

'The Office' was the harvest name for the local pub, only twenty yards from the back door of the farmhouse. Many deals were concluded in the office and, while the hard bargaining continued, we boys would carry on cleaning, bagging and stacking the grain. Looking back through the old visitors' book, I could forget the dust that made me itch and the sweat that stuck it dryly to my skin. It was easier to remember the good times. I hoped our commitment to Bed and Breakfast would give us as much fun and make as many friends.

Our attention turned to schools. The fact that James needed help with his dyslexia was undeniable and now that the B & B concept was firmly planted in a physical state, I was happier. Yet, as we made appointments to visit schools, the injustice of it all grated my conscience. There should be room in the state system to pick up well-understood problems such as dyslexia, to have time for individuals and to have the facilities - academic, practical, and sporting - to bring out these individuals. Sometimes it can, but all too often and especially in rural areas, pupils seem to be pawns in the ongoing game of fund allocation, petty politics and grand schemes that forget the individual. What if we couldn't do Bed and Breakfast or if it didn't work? What about those with no opportunity to do such things and those who have little experience of using their voices and being heard? I turned to a school prospectus that was lying on the table nearby. I knew my growing anger was futile given the timescale that we were working to. I fingered the corner of the glossy cover and vowed to rock the boat one day; but today my duty was at home.

~~~~~~~~~~~~~~~~~~~

Bilton Grange stands in spacious grounds near Rugby. In many ways my image of a prep school, yet far more human. The facilities showed not only money, but careful use of it. Through it all permeated a warmth that grew into a confidently cosy atmosphere. Yes, they had staff trained in dyslexic teaching and, having studied James's reports, felt sure they could teach him to live with and eventually overcome his problem. James was a strong boy for ten and, having played mini-rugby for the county and developed a love of cricket, he was treated as someone who would be a great asset to the school and certainly not one whose learning difficulties would be a liability.

Every parent contemplating boarding school for a child goes through the soul-searching process. In our case, the look on James's face as he absorbed the facilities and saw the possibilities were answer enough. The school needed him, he beamed, and he would be there to score his tries and hit the runs. The doubts, anxiety and downcast lost eyes of recent weeks were gone. Having attended a lowly boarding school in my teens, to say I was envious of the facilities offered here was an understatement.

But this was what fatherhood was about; giving your child the best start you could.

This pompous pride was still filling my oversized head when I heard the headmaster telling Chris that he would like James a term early, to assess his dyslexia and let him settle before the next academic year started in September. James thought the idea marvellous and, of course, they only wanted him early to have his cricketing skills in the school team. We agreed and went home happy, if a little shell-shocked, with the knowledge that our Bed and Breakfast would have to take shape and soon.

We delivered James on a bright and sunny early summer morning and were invited into the headmaster's study as James was whisked away to meet his classmates. Over a coffee, we were told that they found it best if boys went straight into class, where the busy challenge of seeing new faces and attempting new work made the transition easier.

'Ring in a couple of days', said the headmaster, as we left. Our empty numbness was eroded by the growing confidence that we were doing the right thing and at the right school.

The next few days were extremely busy. Guests were increasing with the summer and the preparations for school had put many jobs behind schedule. It was five days before Chris finally rang and spoke to the headmaster.

'You have beaten the record', he began. 'No one has managed to leave it five days before phoning.'

He was not critical or sarcastic and reported that James was fine. On the second night he had considered his own bed might be better and felt a little sad. The dormitory closed ranks with sympathy at which James had declared: 'If you lot will just leave me alone I'll pull myself together.'

He did, and the next day he was playing cricket for the school. A long and happy time at Bilton had begun.

~~~~~~~~~~~~~~~~~~~~

The joy that had overtaken James on his first visit to Bilton threw everything else into shadow. Take a picture from a seemingly well-decorated wall, and you see how in need of attention that wall is. Without wishing to compare my beautiful young daughter to a wall or, indeed, call my son a picture, the effect is the same. Vicki had always been a bright and lovely child and, just as James had received help with reading and writing, she had been supplied with extra books and work to keep her busy.

The school regime change that had suddenly cut off James's help, also denied Vicki her challenge. Equality took on a menacing face, leaving her bored and increasingly rebellious, just as it had left James lost and bewildered. In many ways, her need was as great as his and we had to meet it.

Oxford is well-blessed with private schools for girls. The academic traditions of the city and the wealth of visiting dons have created a feel for learning that seemed right for Vicki.

In the dim and distant past, I had attended a small prep school in north Oxford. It had closed soon after I left and was now the home of a well-respected girl's school. We arrived during the afternoon and were shown into a large, high-ceilinged study. Built as a typical Victorian drawing room, it was now encircled by tall bookcases, which seemed at odds with the new and very functional desk. The headmistress was tall and carried that smile which is designed to relax nervous parents and would-be pupils. It worked. I sat in an old, very comfortable chair as she stimulated the conversation. Vicki's shyness began to dissolve and her short replies became more expressive.

She was only eight but was already rising to the occasion.

'If I have six packets of sweets with three sweets in each packet, costing me a total of 18p, how much is each sweet?', said the headmistress with a suddenness that chilled the air.

Vicki took a breath and looked surprised.

'Well, they would cost you 1p each, but who would buy a packet with only three in it?' A smile spread across the room and we left to see the facilities.

I noticed on the teachers' role that a Miss Clark taught Latin. I could picture an ageing face from years gone by, peering above that traditional Classics teacher's grey suit. Her name had been Miss Clarke, surely it could not be the same!

'Oh, yes', said the headmistress, 'but she doesn't come in every day now. We will meet her later.'

And later, there she was. She was facing the blackboard, her grey hair flowing over the collar of the same grey suit. She turned and was introduced to Vicki,

'...and this is her father, an old pupil of yours, Miss Clarke. I am sure you will remember him.'

As she looked me in the eye, the years seemed to melt away. Mental arithmetic flowed through my brain and came up with twenty-seven. Twenty-seven years since I last stood in this room.

'Yes - you're Bobby, aren't you?!', she said, more as a statement than a question. I wanted to hide and felt much younger than Vicki looked.

Vicki started in the September. The new ring road was being built and the daily journey became an ordeal but academically she prospered. She still took some teachers on as sport and we knew that a larger and more broad education would soon be needed but, for now, she was stimulated and moving forward.

I tried not to let myself mentally combine our school fee commitments. Our first commitment had been to the children and I was happy that we had done right. The money would be found and if ever I felt in doubt, I would picture James going out to bat in his first match or Vicki triumphantly returning with a good exam result. There is nothing like incentive to concentrate the mind.

I have always been amused by those advertisements in national newspapers for 'ambitious and self-motivated people'. What they want, of course, is someone to work their butt off for the good of the company till, burnt out as individuals, they are consigned to the scrap heap. There has never been any fear of me being burnt out, but a trifle more self-motivation wouldn't hurt. The new, streamlined farming system would demand a minimal labour input, except at peak times.

When you are a member of a team of three or four working at a project, a session of Monday morning blues can be picked up by the other team members, and, backside kicked, you soon find yourself redirected into full motivation. I would have to become double-jointed and learn to kick my own backside. The theory of working on my own I found stimulating: the need to be organised without the distraction of outside influences. The practice is very different. I am not an all-rounder and never will be. I would simply have to be successful enough at what I could do, in order to pay for what I couldn't.

The farm was full of possibilities and I could see them coming together. There was the promise of success, of imposing my own personality on a farm that was too much of the past. Like a box of chocolates with too many flavours, I would simply select those that I could enjoy, that felt right, add my love of people and I knew I could develop a whole plan that would work.

I gave us two years to harness the Bed and Breakfast, find new ventures and mature the sheep into a fully profitable operation. At times, the thought made me shake, wake up in a state of hopelessness; then a light would appear at the end of the tunnel, the sun would shine, I would hear the children laugh and anything would be possible.

2

CHAPTER TWO

I remember our first guests as if it were yesterday. It had been an ordinary, uneventful day on the farm. The sheep had only got out once and none had died. The weather had threatened to rain but did not have the energy. It was not warm, but too hot to work in a sweater. Definitely, a truly forgettable day - until I looked along the farmyard and saw a strange car in the drive.

Over the years the sight of such a car has been a bigger stimulant to my imagination than most things I could mention. The immediate expectations that it carried beautifully tanned young ladies or interesting personas would consume my imagination. I looked at my watch, five to five. Yes, time for a cup, and my curiosity led me indoors.

Mr and Mrs Joseph were American, late forties and, as my father would say in his cattle farmer's way, good doers. They carried a cheerful, have-a-good-time look and were seated around the long table in the Breakfast Room, drinking tea with Chris.

'What a lovely house, what lovely rooms!', Mrs Joseph announced, as she sat back in her chair and looked at the high ceiling. The long central beam, lined with studs for hanging sides of bacon in past times, caught her eye. I needed no more encouragement.

'They would be cured in the cellar, soaked in salt in long lead baths, before being brought up here to mature and store.' Already I felt like a museum curator. It was tempting to suggest that a blacksmith fashioned those studs at the same time as Columbus fashioned America. Certainly, a slight stretching of the truth, but tempting all the same.

'Another cup?', asked Chris, bringing me back to the present.

'Oh yes', said Mrs. Joseph, sliding her cup over. Newly arrived that morning, the symptoms of jet lag had been showing on her face, but now the uniquely rejuvenating effect of a timely cup of tea in the old Breakfast Room was shining through. Before anyone gets the wrong idea that our farmhouse is so large that it has a room for every meal, I must explain that the Breakfast Room used to be the kitchen, before the Aga was removed and it was 'updated'. The old dairy room had become the kitchen and the room where we now sat had been intended as a dining room. Chris preferred the title 'Breakfast Room', saying it was less imposing and, anyway, she couldn't cook dinners, only suppers.

'I always invite people to supper, never dinner. Suppers are more relaxed and less is expected. If the food doesn't work out, we can laugh it off. At a full dinner, it would be a disaster.'

Having found Chris's cooking one of the delights of married life, I beg to differ, but have also found it best to let her have her way in domestic matters. It is, and always will be, the Breakfast Room.

It took a while for it to sink in that these were actually paying guests. I was still sitting there when Chris returned from showing them to their room. She was smiling and held out her arms. It had begun. The Josephs will always remain fixed in my memory, not just as our first paying guests, but for their personalities. Larger than life and with a real feeling for the occasion.

That evening, as we all sat around the sitting room fire having a late night cup of coffee, we suggested having a drink - alcoholic of course - to toast our first guests.

'Wonderful idea', said Mrs Joseph, 'but we will drink our bottle first', despatching hubby to their room for a fine bottle of malt.

At that time, we had only two letting rooms, both the size of dormitories, yet traditionally furnished as double rooms. One was our son's room during the holidays and was suitably arranged with all the additions that accompany a ten-year-old boy. Our daughter, Victoria, aged eight, had her own room, decorated to her personal specification with a huge rainbow filling the wall at the head of her bed and a delightful pot of gold at the bottom. This she happily gave up in emergencies. Another double room was next to it and then there was the little sitting room, the smallest room downstairs, with an old French window opening on to our unkempt back garden. Once the tennis changing room when the only polite thing for young Victorian ladies to do was play tennis, it was now a hideaway television room with a fold-out double bed for ultra-emergencies.

The location of the farm is perfect for Bed and Breakfast, only a couple of miles from Blenheim Palace, and en route between Oxford and Stratford. From these early days, the majority of our guests called on the off chance, having asked the postman, shopkeeper, vicar or whomever, and been courteously pointed in our direction. Our imposing seventeenth-century farmhouse often did the trick with Americans and if you could encourage them through the front door and glimpse the copper collection in the Breakfast Room, they rarely even asked the price. European visitors were more circumspect, but once you had broken the ice and convinced them that their English was more than adequate, they relaxed and became very rewarding guests.

In these early days we often had parties of young Germans from around Hamburg during the early summer. The ferry ran from Hamburg to Harwich and they could just about make us on their first day. Young couples and parties escaping the confines of London found us only an hour away and became regular visitors; cosmopolitan with a great desire to have fun. When you tell someone, you are 'doing Bed and Breakfast' they often throw their hands in the air and talk of lost privacy and undesirable guests. The former is all to do with whether you are naturally gregarious or not; the latter has, fortunately, only occurred once.

At that time, we were registered with an agency that advertised abroad and this guest had booked through them to stay with us for a fortnight. Pierre was due to arrive on the Tuesday and did so by ten in the morning. Although we are adjacent to a main tourist route, all towns other than Woodstock are at least ten miles away, so, unless you are on a walking or cycling holiday, some form of transport is essential. Our young man had none, having been dropped off by a very relieved taxi driver.

Chris showed him bus timetables for the village and even offered to take him to Woodstock, from where buses are more frequent.

'I only want to be with you', he would say, staring with menacing, narrow eyes.

I had been out on the farm when he arrived and was made extremely welcome when I came in for lunch. Chris was clearly ill at ease and tried to persuade me to stay in the house and do book work for the afternoon. We ushered Pierre out for a walk around the village and wondered what we were going to do with him for two whole weeks.

We were both out when Vicki returned from school. She had been dropped off at the farm gate and entered the house to find him sitting in the sitting room.

'Who are you?', she asked, already unsettled by his looks. 'Are you a Bed and Breakfast guest? Do my parents know you are here?'

He remained silent and then replied, 'Come and sit here', tapping the arm of his chair. Vicki didn't move but repeated more firmly, 'Do my parents know you are here?'

Again, he tapped his chair and called her over.

'No', she said. 'I think I'll go and see my nan.'

Her grandparents lived just a couple of hundred yards away through the farmyard. She arrived shaken, but determined, as she told her nan the story.

'He looks just like the pictures of sex molesters we are shown at school', she said firmly.

We soon discovered that not only Vicki had been worried, but the whole village was up in arms. His lunchtime visits to the shop and pub had emptied them of customers, many of whom decided not to return.

'He has to go', said Chris, with an adamant but slightly worried voice. When he entered the house, she took the bull by the horns.

'You must go', she said. 'I cannot understand you. Go to London, they will understand you there.'

The bus left thirty minutes later, and we made sure he was on it. Chris returned his money, somehow wanting to be rid of everything to do with him. I wondered whether this episode would put us off but, looking back, its only effect has been to pull us together and make us appreciate our other guests all the more.

After the novelty of our first guests and the horrors of Pierre, a system evolved. Chris was doing the work and I was dropping in to be hospitable. At times I felt truly guilty about this inequality and would offer to push the hoover or make up beds in a spare moment, but such was my inefficiency at these seemingly straightforward operations that Chris would generally smile and send me away.

Only in the kitchen did I feel remotely useful. We had decided that a good farmhouse breakfast was to be one of the hallmarks of our enterprise. Cereals, followed by bacon, egg, sausage, mushrooms, tomatoes, and toast, with variations to suit personal tastes. Cooking breakfast could easily have become a total tie, but with both of us capable of producing a passable meal it was not a problem. I have never progressed beyond the category of assistant chef, but no one has died.

~~~~~~~~~~~~~~~~~~~~

One Sunday morning in April, I was feeling tired but happy. The long lambing season was nearly over and the sun was providing a glorious day. The morning haze was disappearing and the sky peering through. I had checked the ewes and found two pairs of newly born lambs in good health. Yes, I would enjoy my breakfast.

Eleanor, a fine girl of seventeen, whose interest in farming her parents may genuinely blame on us, peered round the Breakfast Room door.

'Another ewe lambing, she's alright but needs time. Can I leave her to you, I'm playing Young Farmer Hockey...' and she was gone.

Sheep may seem the same to most people but, as with people, they are all individuals. They have their own foibles and ways, and these must be observed.

We had two pairs of guests that morning. A middle-aged couple with a great feeling for the country and a young newspaper journalist and his wife.

'Will she lamb soon; may we see?'

I looked across the table at Chris, remembering when the village playgroup had arrived the previous year immediately after the birth of a dead lamb. This is where reality and romance must meet.

'Yes, I think so, there shouldn't be any trouble', I said, as I rose from the table.

Then I added, 'Without meaning to be intrusive, I don't recommend you come if you think you're pregnant. We haven't any obvious problems, but it's never wise for a pregnant girl to visit pregnant ewes and new lambs. Various infections to which the sheep may be immune or resistant can affect expectant humans.'

Whether I hoped this information would deter our guests or not, I don't know but, if I did, I was to be disappointed. They seemed to rise from their seats with renewed vigour and followed the safari to the lambing shed.

All seemed well; the presentation was good and any second a mighty heave from mum would propel another fine strong lamb into the world. The heave came but the lamb didn't. It appeared totally wedged in the pelvis and soon a second lamb, anxious to be born was trying to push its legs into the confusion. I immediately wished I had not invited our guests. The middle-aged lady was now crouching by the ewe's head, comforting her with gentle words, which became less and less gentle to my ears as problems evolved into potential disaster.

'Now, my dear,' she whispered, stroking its long white nose, 'it's going to be alright, just hang on a little longer.' The ewe responded by looking her in the eye, taking a deep breath and settling into virtual sleep.

After nearly an hour the first lamb was hauled into the world, all life squeezed from it during its hard delivery. The second lamb followed in a similar state. Well, at least the ewe is alright. The thought was premature. With an almighty and belated push, she exerted pressure on her uterine muscles, which had been bruised giving birth. The pressure was too much and she prolapsed. Much pushing and stitching, disinfecting and a hefty dose of antibiotics later, she was back together but, as she lay there, head still cradled in the lady's arms, she ran out of life and passed to the great pasture in the sky.

'You can sleep now', said the lady, running her hand down the sheep's nose for the last time. As if in unison, a single tear ran down her face. The pure simplicity had got to her too.

It was all very sad, yet somehow still romantic. All that could have been done had been done and if ever the newspaper journalist needed to use experience to pass comment on farmers, perhaps he would remember this. As to the lady, she would certainly remember today and know that the real romance of farming is all about real life and, sometimes, death.

~~~~~~~~~~~~~~~~~~~~

April is, without doubt, my favourite month. The long, hard winter is finally coming to an end and the reality of the new season is forcing its way into the world. That February day, although only two months back, has hatched a confidence and a hope, which the Easter sunshine is making real and sustainable. So much of this hope is based on the conviction that the farm and what it stands for is worth retaining, worth fighting for.

A few years ago, Chris and I were party guests of friends in the legal profession. A mix, from lowly barristers to eminent judges, with us as the only farmers in sight. After several short and shallow conversations, I became engrossed with a judge who found rural life beyond his comprehension.

'How many acres do you own and what is it worth?', he asked, as if cross-examining some confused witness. I did a few sums and surprised myself.

'Well, how can you afford to farm it, when you could live comfortably off the investment?', he questioned.

There was no logical answer to this question. I could have mentioned history, tradition, love, care and the future. I might have brought in the role of custodian, but I knew I would have been speaking to deaf ears. And was he wrong! Like some trainee priest undergoing temptation, I had to believe that I was right. Just as new crops and new ways made every season that bit different to the last, I had to feel I was not just digging in, head in the sand, but evolving towards the future.

As I walk out on an April morning, I feel a joy that no investment, no financial security could ever give. I want to run as a young boy, down to the river where the pike lie sleepily. I want to cut a willow wand from a nearby tree, take the wire from my pocket and make a snare. I want to catch that pike and see it thrashing on the bank and the trout flash safely upstream. It is not just the natural cruelty of a young boy, nor the wish to save the beautiful trout from this freshwater shark, but the feeling of belonging and of taking part. It is the need to find a way of keeping pace with all around, to fend off the sharks of the world.

Sharing makes most things in life better and easier, and it is easier to share on a sunny day. Sometimes people and events detract from the goal, sometimes they are an essential part of it. Increasingly, the latter dominates as spring takes over from the doubts of winter.

It is nearly lunch time. I sit back in my chair and let the sunshine stream through the window and play on my face. I close my eyes and feel the blame evaporate as mist on a summer morning. I am by the river and we are looking for the pike, none of the symbolism now, but true escapism, memories from the past.

There are six of us, all wearing polaroids to cut out the glare; three on this bank and three on the other. One on each bank carries a willow with wire snare attached, two stand upstream of him and two down.

At Easter, the large female fish move upstream to spawn. They become sluggish and heavy, basking in the spring sun. They often seem out of place, too big for the river, as they shimmer, hardly moving in a quiet current. I make a noose large enough to fit over the head of the fish and lower it slowly into the river, letting it drift in the current, in front of and down to the fish. A bit deeper, deeper still, as the stick breaks the surface causing ripples and disturbing my view. I lift it slowly, the fish is gone. Someone upstream has seen it and points it out. The same procedure, the same concentration, till at last the noose slides over the head and slowly, slowly back. Then, with muscles tensed, I pull up and forward, feel it grip the fish and lift. The willow takes the strain and the fish is soon flashing silver on the bank. A cheer, the battle won. I hear a voice.

'Bob, wake up, it's time for lunch.' Chris is beside me.

'You were dreaming.' I look about me, partly by the river, partly in the room; partly in the past and partly in the future.

'Are you ready for lunch?' I suddenly feel very hungry.

'Yes, fishing is a hungry business', I say aloud, but unheard as Chris disappears from the room.

Bank holidays soon became known for the rush of guests they brought with them, just as the week following became known for its absolute quietness, as guests fought their way home or saved their pennies. Sometimes, special events would give a special personality to a holiday. A few years ago, in our pre-Bed and Breakfast days, we would have loaded up with sheep and driven down to Somerset for the late May holiday to take in the Bath and West show. The early May break can still involve a similar trip to Newark for the Notts County Show but, increasingly, we knew that our commitment to Bed and Breakfast must include the 'stay at home' factor.

We could not afford to miss these popular times. We were adamant, however, that we must also have fun where we could; our fun would be their fun, we conveniently told ourselves, and always kept our eyes open for dual opportunities.

Over the years, we have made many friendships which have been based around our farming - and especially the sheep breeding - but which have then broadened to take in other interests. Some of my happiest memories involve cricket. And so, as we prepared ourselves for the forthcoming late May holiday and the touring cricket team which was coming to stay and play, amongst other sides, my own invitation team, I knew that we were in for a stay-at-home holiday par excellence!

John, a fine hockey player, who was fifteen years my senior and proud of the fact that he hadn't touched a cricket bat since leaving school, was firmly in situ at the farmhouse table, replete after an excellent supper. We were debating malts when the phone rang. It was a sheep-breeding friend from Norfolk called Chris, a stalwart of the season and captain of the touring team due in May.

'You must be preparing for our visit, how about some practice to make sure you are ready?' He seemed to take my silence as agreement.

'We meet in Southend at one tomorrow', he said, as if this should be more than ample notice. I resisted the predictable exhortation.

'I'll see what I can do and ring back.' I turned to John.

'Are you game for a laugh?'

He took minimal persuasion and so, having told Chris that I had worked miracles and that he should do the same, we planned our route.

The next day, a sleepy ribbon of houses, separated from the oozing tidal mud by a straight and very boring road, led us to the meeting place, needless to say, a pub. It was also no surprise that we were the first there. Several drinks later they started arriving, dribbling in more like an army in retreat than a band of fighting men ready for conflict.

As the evening came, their energies improved and we made our way to a local restaurant for dinner. Recently re-upholstered in gaudy lights and bright plastic, it did not carry a high star rating. Triviality floated in the air, coaxing fun from the most unlikely members and lunacy from some. John found fault with the wine and Chris disappeared in search of the very attractive waitress who had just served him his soup. It was then that we discovered the restaurant was owned by a very fit ex-boxer with some fearsome-looking associates.

Our apprehension deepened when we realised that the waitress was his wife. Chris was retrieved intact and we made a tactical withdrawal with John last to leave, still claiming the claret was corked.

'Apprehension' was an apt description as the team readied itself for its first match the next day. The famous old garrison ground, host to many county encounters, seemed destined for disappointment. The sun broke through as we arrived, shining brightly on the newly painted white balustrade that surrounded the dignified old pavilion. The words of the ancient hymn came back to me: 'Pavilioned in splendour and girded with praise'. I doubted if it could be a true description of the day ahead.

Although I had played with Chris on several occasions, the rest of the team were new to me. The captain won the toss and elected to bat first, a sign of confidence. I was asked to open the batting with a tall, spectacled lad called Phil. I use the term 'lad' relatively; though nearer fifty than forty, he was still one of the youngsters of the team. He played several good shots till he missed a ball that happened to be straight and was out. Chris came in next, exuding confidence. I played several risky shots, which I got away with. Chris showed no emotion but wandered down the pitch, ostensibly levelling some hypothetical bumps, 'gardening'. He continued and met me mid-pitch, looked up and spoke as some country squire.

'Steady down, old boy. We're the last batsmen, make a bit of a game of it.' I tried not to look surprised and levelled a fictitious bump of my own.

'What about the other eight players?', I replied, almost as an aside.

'They're only here for the beer, now get your head down.'

I did as I was told and was finally out for forty. Chris went on to make fifty and we were all out for a hundred and ten. I accepted his judgement for the rest of the tour.

That evening the whole team had light heads; the next morning they were much heavier. We knew we had escaped lightly against a very good team and meant to celebrate. As we wandered down the long, straight road that separated what was euphemistically termed 'the sea front' from the avenues of uninteresting semi-detached retirement homes, John stopped dead in his tracks with a grin on his face, which I knew meant trouble. Several seasons playing hockey together had prepared me for his well-developed sense of humour and acute love of the practical joke.

Adjacent to one of these cul-de-sac avenues was a heap of road signs left from a recently completed roadworks scheme. I could see John working out his plan, partly concentrating on perfecting it, partly resisting it - as should a rising light of the legal profession. The plan won and he looked up and down the road to check it was all clear.

'Bob, move these bollards to the middle of the road and put this sign over there.' John distributed some the other way, nimbly and quickly creating order from the untidy heap. Order was soon to be a thing of the past.

Before the next car came into view, a diversion had appeared, directing cars from both directions down the same cul-de-sac. We stood back to admire the effect of his work, before wandering nonchalantly on down the road through the growing chaos of irate motorists.

That evening we went ten-pin bowling between visitations to various local hostelries. The next morning, breakfast and the match that followed became a dull blur. I believe I kept wicket, as I was fitter than the regular keeper, and that we narrowly lost. Of greater importance was that I discovered the team to be of true cavalier proportions, brimming with talent, though not especially good at cricket. If these were typical of the side that Chris was bringing for the Bank Holiday, I knew what would be expected of me.

To many, a game of Sunday cricket on the village green is a thing of sleepy poetry. As old as the game itself, it is an escape from the rat race of the modem world where two uneven, often untalented sides while away the heat of a summer's day, filling the time between Sunday lunch and pub opening time in a state where competitive spirit is only rarely allowed to rear its ugly head. The desire to achieve a significant win is diluted, not only by the pre-match beer, but also by a traditional caring for the underdog; after all, they might have us on the rack next year.

The philosophy of not losing being vastly more important than winning has been the backbone of the draw; a uniquely cricketing state of mind and body. Beneath all this camaraderie and tradition, however, things do not just happen. The pitch must be prepared, the team chosen, the tea arranged and all within the laid back, unpressured attitude that is village cricket.

After many phone calls I had finally been asked to arrange the match for the Bank Holiday Monday. Chris didn't want any ordinary side, but an invitation team, incorporating as many of the local characters he had met with us on shoot days or sheep visits as possible, mingled, if necessary, with a few hardened cricketers. They must be able to join in the pre-match pub lunch in the right spirit, look appropriate on the field in mostly-white kit, be able to laugh at their own lack of talent and fitness but be just good enough to force the important result, a draw.

I knew that the team I had played with at Southend was not a true reflection of his club's normal strength. I had heard reports of high scores, gifted young players and a surfeit of victories this season, which seemed at odds with the sort of team Chris had asked me to find.

A big problem is knowing the actual talents of your own team. A friend who I may have met through farming or just being a neighbour may claim to only play occasionally, when he is, in fact, an ex-county player who can score fifty in half a dozen overs. Another may say he is a fast bowler when, in reality, he only *wanted* to be a fast bowler and proves as likely to hit the pavilion as he is the stumps.

Amidst the negotiations and accepted balance of team selection, which finally came down to finding anyone who could make up numbers on the day, was the task of organising the pitch. I started with total confidence and the misconception that I merely needed to find the captain of the village team, check my understanding that the pitch was not being used that day to be correct and then hire it.

Having played for the village team for several years I knew the captain well and found him mowing the pitch. He confirmed that there was no match that day but first he must check that no late fixture had been arranged and that the football club did not want it. If that proved satisfactory, I would have to find the field committee and hire it from them. Of course, I would still need to decide with the groundsman about the cost of the actual wicket and would I need the pavilion? I looked confused. The pavilion came under the hall committee and would need to be booked separately, as would the cricket kit from the cricket club and tea-making facilities from the ladies in charge.

I was amazed that so much bureaucracy could be achieved in so small a village, especially when most of these committees were made up of the same people. I satisfied myself that this was the uniquely British spirit that had built an empire and then lost it.

As the day approached, I felt quietly confident that my team was of the right balance: a few cricketers, mixed with hopefuls and 'has-beens', but all characters fully able to laugh at themselves. I had met with every committee and felt sure no more could possibly exist. I prayed for a dry day.

The players made their way the hundred yards or so from the pub to the cricket field in assorted groups. Some erred on the side of discretion and took a lift, but it was well after start time before the umpires made their way to the middle and balanced the bails on the gleaming white stumps. Still uncertain about my team's real strength and in the face of growing reports about the opposition, extracted during weak moments over lunch, I put the touring team into bat.

Big Billy was a fearsome character, his mighty frame increased by the many bottles of pilsner consumed during lunch, and when he hit the second ball to the boundary with a resounding crack of willow on leather, the situation looked ominous. Young Kevin was bowling and appeared overcome by the power of Billy. The final ball of the over saw the nerves that had been building in the bowler take over. The ball arched in a totally accidental loop and descended towards Billy with pinpoint accuracy. His mighty blow was too soon and the ball, somehow avoiding his massive frame, landed on the top of the middle stump, cascading the bails high into the air. Our forefathers would have considered it the perfect 'donkey drop'.

Accidents such as this early in a cricket match can become markers of destiny. The visitors struggled to a score of a hundred and fifty, well below their best and, as we enjoyed the sponge cakes, filled with strawberries and deep cream and passed the warm lardy cake along the table, I thought things could be a lot worse. Malcolm, an old school friend who was playing his first game for eighteen months and Graham, new to the village, were given the honour of opening our innings, as the team concentrated on some serious drinking.

After a while, someone enquired about the score. The match had somehow slipped from our consciousness and no one could remember hearing anyone get out. We discovered that we had scored fifty and, with the two lads performing brilliantly, returned to socialising. A ripple of applause witnessed the century partnership and the knowledge that few of the team would need to bat relieved the floodgates that had held several players in relative sobriety. That we won by nine wickets was a travesty of the balance of natural talents held by the two teams, but I didn't let it stop me heckling Chris about bringing a decent team next year. A change is as good as a rest, they say, and cricket will never be quite the same.

~~~~~~~~~~~~~~~~~~~~~~~

As Easter moved into May, and May into June, we began to feel like Bed and Breakfast professionals. The early nervousness developed into bland over-confidence. We soon found that a busy weekend could turn into several days without even an enquiry. That as soon as you had taken a single person into a family room, the perfectly sized family would come to the door. One of the most interesting factors was the mixing of groups staying at the same time. It is unfair to make generalisations based on nationality, but the effect of sharing a bathroom, which was necessary in those early days, and sitting round the same long table for breakfast, which we still do, had interesting results.

One memorable week in June we had three groups staying. An American lady from Texas with her son, an elderly American couple and a young, middle-aged pair from Germany, with dry humour and perfect English. I had previously been under the misapprehension that Texas was merely a state of the U.S.A. I was soon informed that it was THE state, around which all America revolved, and that sizes had new and awe-inspiring dimensions there. The serving of milk at breakfast in a pint jug was a source of utter amazement. 'We always serve milk by the gallon.'

We try to eat our breakfast with the guests and use the opportunity to talk freely to them, making them at home and answering any questions, from 'Where is the nearest castle?' to 'How do you play cricket?' This morning was the first with this blend of American and German guests. Whatever anyone said was soon countered by larger and more impressive stories from our Texan lady.

The sport evolved into who could exaggerate more and still be topped before the subject was changed. The son realised the rules of the sport and joined in, unless his mother went truly over the top, when he would sit as tall as his sixteen years would allow and tell his mother to behave. It transpired that dad had been intending to accompany the duo but the pressure of work had kept him at home. We soon realised why. The elderly American couple sat quietly by in a very dignified way. When the mother and son had left the room, the man came up and said, 'I'm sorry, not all Americans are like that.' We discovered that this dignified old man had been second in command of the first moon shot. His gentle wit and broad knowledge acted as a vivid contrast to his compatriot. America is certainly a big country.

We decided early on not to do evening meals. The range of good restaurants in the area seemed to make it unnecessary and we felt we needed some freedom to ourselves. Many guests, especially those who had travelled long distances, used a nearby restaurant and were back by soon after nine. We could then invite them to join us for coffee and many interesting discussions developed.

One guest was head of education for Westphalia in Germany. Having just sent James to boarding school and Vicki to a prep school in Oxford, education was fresh in our minds. There can be few better ways of breaking the European divide than such a relaxed occasion.

I have often wondered why farmhouses are so popular for Bed and Breakfast guests. Perhaps familiarity breeds contempt, but their corridors always seem chilly to me and the paintwork in need of another coat. It must be their character, a lovely way of describing a one-off building, which all farmhouses are, in need of attention. I think all these have some effect, as does the imposing size of the building and its large, reassuring rooms. But, above all these, it is a real home and hub of a real farm. I know of some 'farmhouses' that no longer have farms attached, and their feel and atmosphere have gone; they have been strangled, the tourniquet fitted, and all that is left is the shell.

Few people in this overpopulated world of ours, from any country, will not claim to have come from farming ancestry within the last two or three generations. A visit to a working farm becomes a pilgrimage without the mess. A world so different from their daily rat race that the changes compliment the illusion. For a short while they can wallow in their imagined nostalgia. It gives them room to wander with the sun on their back and the crystal-clear stream bubbling at their feet. Fleetingly, they can be a country squire; a sense of belonging and purpose may follow, and problems can easily fall into the slots that have been eluding them. The world can become a simpler and far finer place. Romance perhaps, but where are we without romance?

Breakfast is taken to fit the wishes of individual groups and can be a straggled affair lasting over two hours, or a rapid feast and a rush to the plane. In the summer, I rise with the sun, or nearly, and check that all is well with the sheep before I come in for breakfast. I am soon met with enquiries as to the breed of the sheep in this field and the health of the ram in that. The embryonic squires are settling their minds that all is right and straight on their acres. They will soon be able to drive off and visit the picture postcard of the tourist manuals with a clear conscience.

Sometimes, conversation can develop beyond the romance and find itself in the real world. A vast number of people still think farmers should wear funny hats and chew straw. The incorporation of the same market forces in this idyllic setting as these level-headed guests use every day in their offices, they find difficult to accept. In many ways, I have only myself to blame. Nostalgia and romance are, and must be used as a market force, as far as Bed and Breakfast guests are concerned, whilst the sheep, corn, and anything else the farm grows must likewise be governed by the market.

CHAPTER THREE

The house is the fulcrum of the farm. Built in 1639, the year before the civil war broke out, it has been the family home for over a hundred and fifty years. Occupying the prime position in the village it is and always has been a complete farmhouse. I'm not saying that some farmhouses are incomplete, in that they lack walls or a roof, but that they were originally built as small dwellings and have been extended to their present size as facilities demanded or prosperity allowed. The result is often an unplanned mish-mash of corridors and small rooms on different levels, giving what visitors rather than inhabitants would call 'character'.

The character of our farmhouse comes from its balance. Unaltered since its construction, the ceilings are high, the rooms large, and a feeling exists that I have found in few other houses. It only has two reception rooms and four bedrooms, though the attic is large and full of potential. It is certainly no mansion and retains a homeliness and need for people. In my grandfather's day it was a house for one maid. Things had obviously been going downhill, for a photo taken at the turn of the century shows four, but such are the times. I can remember visiting my grandfather in my early youth. The drawing room was to the left from the hall as you entered the house and the fire was always out, or nearly so.

Memories of a cold room and of rushing, as soon as I could, back through the hall to the kitchen beyond, stand prominently in my mind. Bathy would be standing by the old black range, heaped high and glowing red.

'Come here, my duck, and warm yourself.' Standing just four feet seven inches in her worn slippers, she looked warm and comfortable. A genuine cockney, she had a soft spot for all children. I picture her busy making the harvest tea; local bread, thin sliced and made into well-peppered tomato sandwiches, dry dough cake and tea. The tea was something very different: weak, milky, poured into an old Cider bottle and wrapped in newspaper to keep warm.

'I know how you make it', Michael, the young tractor driver, would say as he collected it from the back door.

'You put the tea pot in one corner of the room and throw the tea leaves at it from the other, you old witch', before running for the safety of the farmyard.

On the seemingly high windowsill lived a tin, where Bathy kept a supply of toffee that I eagerly attacked as I warmed and chatted. From the old dairy room beyond the kitchen, a flight of stairs led to Bathy's bedroom above.

The village shop is also in the middle of the village, on the far side of the central ring from which all roads radiate. As I returned from errands for Bathy, walking round the elevated pavement and back up towards the house, it towered above me, imposing and looking larger than I knew it to be. It would almost have been frightening had my love of it not been so great. Even today, the look of the old house as I climb the hill towards it, with clouds rushing above its stone roof leaving me almost dizzy, could be from a Hitchcock film.

On level ground again, I can remember the large elm tree that stood by the gate, the barrelled water butt nearby and the old summer house. All are gone, yet the house has that strong, secure feel that makes it not only the family house, but the rock on which it is based. As it has become increasingly the centre, not only of our family history, but also of our hopes and aspirations for the future, I have felt myself pulled in two directions. An old family house can easily take on the air of a church; not religiously, but in that it means so many things to so many people. What does it mean to me? At times, a millstone, as the water finds its way through the holey roof or an east wind reminds us all that the heating is minimal. But love needs to hurt sometimes and, if I had to describe in one word my feelings for the old building that holds so much, I would have to say love.

Traditional, yes; romantic, certainly; but through this, the house becomes not just history or a group of rooms between four walls and under a roof. It is a living entity that needs not only memories but also challenges to keep it vibrant and alive. Our new challenge for it was to be more than our family home; to extend it to the world outside through Bed and Breakfast, hospitality days, fishing and more people-related ideas still in their embryonic stage. It had to be our link between the traditional farm and the new world, which seemed to be teetering all around. The old house gave me confidence.

'I'm glad you're here and strong enough to hold me.' I spoke aloud as I lay in the bath and looked at the shapes made by the peeling paint on the ceiling. 'With you, I will find the answer', and I slipped gently lower into the water.

I felt that, in many ways, the world was lost in its race to nowhere and needed us more than ever. I knew that, however our new enterprises evolved, we had to share this historic confidence and romance with a world that had become inconsequential and loveless. Why did I feel so cocky? I had only a heap of stone and wood and a bundle of ideas. But, as I looked about me, I knew I had a great deal more.

The Breakfast Room is not large and is dominated by the old pine dresser against one wall and the huge pine fireplace surround, the home of the copper and brass collection, on another. An old, carved oak cupboard reaches to the ceiling with imposing gargoyles staring down from its prominent upper section. The large mahogany table fills the centre of the room and I am often amazed that there is still enough space for twelve people to sit around it. As the first signs of autumn show themselves with a raw, penetrating feel to the wind, the fire in the breakfast room is lit and a room of natural warmth becomes truly cosy, as only a farmhouse kitchen can.

'I'll bring some more logs and then I'll be in for breakfast', I call to Chris, as I stack an armful of split timber beside the roaring blaze. A few moments later, wellingtons removed, I am sitting in the high-backed chair and stretching my toes towards the fire. A deep conversation between the crackle of the fire and the distinctive, drifting scent of cooking bacon lulls me into total relaxation. I find the energy to twist my head and look at the clock, five to nine.

'Those poor, poor people in their cars fighting their way into London', I murmur, as I snuggle deeper into the wings of my chair.

What makes a room and gives it character? In a room like this, every piece has its own history. How these individual pieces gel together with the attitudes that live there to create its final ambience is as obscure as life.

Let us take the old, carved oak cupboard. Standing some eight feet high and four feet wide, it demands respect. Initially, it seems settled like an old man with his pipe in his favourite chair. Then you think of its age, its passage through many lands over several centuries and you feel deeply humble and privileged to look and run your fingers over its fine detail. The respect demanded earlier takes on a more personal, familiar attachment. It now entices admiration, for the piece and the man whose hands lovingly carved each section all those years ago. That its doors are flung open many times a day and that most of the daily china looks upon it as home, does not detract from the natural romance.

The old dresser opposite is, at first glance, less interesting. As with much pine furniture, fashion had imposed many layers of paint over the years and it wasn't until we decided to have it dipped and this paint removed that its full beauty was literally brought to light.

It came out well enough in two sections, revealing the rough-cut flag stones and original builder's dust beneath, and showing it to be as old as the house itself. We waited to hear from the dipping man that it was ready for collection. After a time, we contacted him and received a very guarded reply. It was now in many pieces, the original joints somehow dissolving during treatment and the back wood having disappeared completely. With much painstaking work it came together, until it reached its present beauty. Although now complete, the dresser will always lack the worldliness of the cupboard opposite. The carved sections linking the ceiling-high shelves somehow have a mother-like smile. Yet the dresser, looking directly at the cupboard, seems to be saying,

'Never mind, you may have seen the world, but I was here when you were little more than an acorn and don't you forget it'.

On the wall between them hangs a painting of the last Oxfordshire wagon the farm used, standing proudly before traditional round ricks of unthrashed grain. Ricks and a wagon as timeless as the furniture that surrounds them, but here in this very farmyard, and painted in the year I was born. The painting only measures 2 ft by 1.5ft, yet brings the infinity of time and place back to the here and now and somehow justifies my existence.

The fire surround is not naturally beautiful. It is of similar wood to the dresser and obviously built to match it, yet can never find its balance or symmetry. But add some copper and brass and it comes to life.

The copper brings out the red of the pine and glistens gently. The brass, blended at random, gives variation and contrast. Each piece different and unique, but working in harmony to create the overall effect that strikes you as you enter from the hall.

'Just look at that fire!', Edna said, as she took her third step into the house. The door to the breakfast room stood open, beckoning. Ahead, the hallway looked narrow in contrast to the width of the fireplace, which, with its natural wood and glowing metal, seemed large and impressive. Edna was drawn in.

'This is a real kitchen, I can feel the age, can't you Bernard?' Bernard followed, weighed down with luggage and struggling for breath. He inhaled more deeply than necessary - the effect of the room?

'Yes', he sighed, 'I can feel the age', and smiled. Here, with the fire burning on a chill autumn evening, you feel cossetted but never smothered. So much history with so much to share, you are never lonely either.

When we moved into the house and my parents decamped to a smaller, more modern and easily maintained home, we had two sitting rooms, side by side. It had always been our intention to make them into one room and one late summer's day it happened.

We had only moved in a week previously and these rooms had been left bare for decoration. I was going to play in the last cricket match of the season and my mother-in-law had come to visit. When I returned in the failing light of early evening, it seemed smoke was gently coming in through the open windows of the rooms. It was not smoke, but dust, and, as it cleared, two very dirty human shapes with very wicked eyes emerged.

'Well, we were going to do it and we happened to find this sledgehammer, and ...'

Fortunately, the partition wall was only a stud wall and carried no load. It had come out very well and already one could see the natural symmetry of the windows and the balance from which the room would benefit. It had two fireplaces, but one was at right angles to the other and so different that they would complement, rather than detract from each other.

'What do you think?', said Chris, grinning at her mother and now relieved that I was showing no anger.

'Well', I said thoughtfully, 'I have seen smaller village halls.'

We never regretted the action and, now that the room has mellowed, it is full of character. At thirty-six feet long, I had to take out a special loan to carpet it, but at Christmas, with the tree shining brightly, complemented by the roar of the fire and the reflections of a full length mirror, it really comes to life.

There is something about a large room that blows the cobwebs from your mind. We were told we would find so large a room cold and draughty, yet we have found it neither. The large, open fire is very efficient, and it always amuses us to watch the circle of chairs pushed gently but purposefully back as the evening develops and the heat builds up.

The flexibility of a large room is often under-appreciated. You need not use it all if you don't want to, but it's very handy to have a room where you can seat fifty to eat or hold a party. Previously, only one of the rooms had been used regularly, leaving the other to become damp and neglected.

That was seven years ago. The large room has become a natural part of the house, as if it had always been here. It will never have the intimacy of the Breakfast Room; its furniture is smaller and less imposing, with the chairs arranged in two semi-circles around the two fireplaces. Its strength is in its quiet dignity and potential power, like an old man-o'-war gently rolling at anchor. It is always there, waiting. For being alone or being with fifty others, its character is reassuring.

In the beginning we had only enough for one semi-circle of chairs. The furnishings of the smaller, more modern home that was now my parents' had been left for them or were incompatible. The two armchairs were both recliners; one had been bought by Chris as a present for me several Christmases before, the other she had bought for herself to keep me company. Later, on a visit to Witney, she noticed that two similar chairs still remained in the shop.

'How much do you want for the chairs?', she asked the man in the tall, lean body and pin stripe suit. He looked at the label, 'Two-hundred pounds each, madam', he replied in a firm, precast voice.

'Oh, you misunderstand', she swept on, 'I know you have been asking that price for some time, but they are still here. They're not selling, are they? I'll give you a hundred each for the pair.'

The young man seemed ruffled, unprepared for anything but a yes or a no. 'I'll ask the manager', and he retreated to the office. The manager finally emerged.

'Ah, madam, did you not buy two similar chairs a while back?'

'I'll give you marks for memory,' Chris thought to herself, 'now how many will you earn for reality!'

'Yes', she said, returning to the present, 'and I will offer you two-hundred pounds for the remaining pair, you must want them gone by now.'

'Ah, Madam...', he began again.

'You irritating man,' Chris thought.

'The best I can do is three hundred the pair, a significant discount I'm sure you'll agree.' Chris gave a sad smile, moved towards the door, took a card from her pocket and turned back to the man.

'No, two hundred for the pair is plenty. This is my number, ring me when you want me to collect them.' Six months later, the man rang and we now have two semi-circles of chairs.

On the first floor, three of the bedrooms face south and one, the old maid's room, faces north. The bathroom, once another maid's room had been chosen to be converted when internal bathrooms first became necessary, as it had been the smallest bedroom. It also faces north and is at the diametrically opposite corner of the house to the water heating system, which was installed at the same time as the original conversion. These two factors ensured that any heat originally added to the water had long since dispersed by the time it trickled sluggishly from the tap. The bathroom is still in the same place, but the water system has now been upgraded.

'The forty-year plan' was the phrase frequently used to describe our ongoing list of changes and improvements. In our early days of residence, Chris and I started with the windows. Many were showing years of neglect and the main kitchen window appeared twisted and was permanently open, its top six inches blocked with old newspaper and held up with a wooden batten. We employed a local carpenter who systematically checked every window, repairing and making good. They were all old bow windows and most of the sash cords had long since broken. It became quite a novelty to be able to open any window and know it would stay that way without suddenly decapitating anyone.

'You can age a house by its sash windows, you know', said Pip, the involuntary village carpenter. In his late forties and a hard-hitting member of the village cricket team, his age was only given away by his greying hair, which, when he smiled, seemed in sharp contrast to his tall, hungry looks. Forced to find some way of supporting his wife and two sons, Pip's training as a carpenter had directed him away from his natural path, that of blissful idleness. He had developed lethargy to a high standard and was proud of it, and the task of gently checking every window had the possibilities for such solitary slowness that he was happy.

'Can you find much damage?', I asked, having discovered him in an upstairs room.

'No, not too bad, need new sashes and the sills are past their prime, but the main windows are fine. Look at these bars', he continued, pointing at and then running his finger and thumb down the thin bars that separated the panes. 'You wouldn't get timber like that today, not straight enough in the grain for a piece so fine.'

A pride was showing through the lethargy - though he wouldn't admit it.

'It's good none of these are damaged or I don't know what I'd do. They're some of the oldest I've seen.'

'How do you know?', I said, settling myself on the corner of the bed in readiness for a long, drawn-out answer.

'Most sash windows have little trap doors to open for replacing the chord; some had long wooden plates held by screws, but at first they just nailed them up. They must have been sure they would last for ever. But they didn't!', he uttered, almost triumphantly. 'They only lasted three hundred and fifty years!' He held the frayed end of an old chord and, smiling, shook his head in mock condemnation.

We left the kitchen window until last, dreading major problems and anticipated expense. The batten was removed and the old newspaper gingerly taken out. Old newspapers are always more interesting than new ones and very good for helping with dates. These had been delivered twenty years before. Twenty years blocking up a window! I shook my head with the thought but was distracted by the sound of the old window being opened and shut, flowing freely in its runners. It was not twisted or warped and therefore had no reason to be open, so it was closed and left.

Without a good sash cord to balance it, the window gradually slid back until it settled as it had been, but with an even larger gap. The realisation slowly came to me. The sash cord had broken, allowing the window to slide open. As a temporary measure, it had been wedged shut but the selected batten had been six inches too short and, instead of cutting one six inches longer, the offending gap had simply been stuffed with the first thing to come to hand, the daily paper. I always said my father should have had an honorary degree in bodging!

The windows, big Sitting Room and kitchen took up most of our time in the first six years and, as one project was completed, so another became evident, either physically or in Chris's imagination. Love is blind, but my affection for the old house did not hide its obvious need for more attention.

As I sat in my chair, leaning on the Breakfast Room table and pensively running my finger up and down my now cold cup of tea early that summer morning, I felt released. It was as if the house knew we were making an effort and wanted to mother me. There was so much more to do and so little money with which to do it. I knew that before this year was out, radical detail would have to be added to the bones of the 'forty year plan' but, with the house still full of guests, the table to be laid and a farm waiting for me beyond these comforting walls, now was not the time.

4

CHAPTER FOUR

The river Glyme flows gently through the farm and onwards, feeding the lake at Blenheim and eventually into the Thames. In the frequent summer droughts that hit this Cotswold brash land, the river declines to little more than a weed-infested trickle. Yet it never goes dry and, somehow, its wild brown trout evade the visiting herons and survive. Years ago, it was renowned for its freshwater crayfish before plague put an end to them. The road takes just a mile to link our village with the next, but the river takes three, such are its meanders along the way.

The valley forms the southern boundary of the farm and the land slopes gently down to it, its southern aspect exaggerating the drought. As a productive farming unit, it has severe limitations. The soil is shallow and very stony. As an aesthetically pleasing wildlife haven, however, it is unequalled. Am I biased? Of course. My family has been here since the 1820s and it is in my bones.

In those early days, the village had its own water mill with an artificial course to give a head of water to drive the wheel. Long since redundant, the mill stream remained flowing for over a mile up stream above the village. Three years ago, with the banks of the old stream breaking down and destroying the meadow beyond, we decided to form a lake using the head of water in the mill stream. It now extends to over two acres and, stocked with trout, it offers superb fishing. A landing stage serves a small dinghy, which can be sailed round the three islands and already the kingfishers and ducks, geese and waders have come to revel in the teeming insect life. It has become a favourite with guests wanting a gentle, off-road, summer evening stroll. Part of the being of the farm, it can show in a short time the benefits of tranquillity, the setting sun blazing gloriously to the west as the wildlife world comes to life in an array of sound.

I look upon the lake as one of nature's delightful accidents. Nature's because, although man-made, it had the feel of returning water from the close confines of the mill race to the lower and nearly original path of the water. Accident, because it was never really planned, but grew from a small idea and a digger driver's imagination.

It had been July and a very dry July too. The farm had already lost its early summer youthfulness and taken on the mantle of an old man with a terminal disease. The heat had encouraged verdant growth in and around the stream, the flooded meadow standing out as an oasis, the brightness of the green showing across the valley, as though the artist had used the wrong colour on his canvas. Only at the very highest point was it possible to cross the meadow and, even then, slowly, in long wellingtons.

Why didn't I leave it, let it return to the wide boggy expanse it had no doubt been in centuries past? I have often wondered. I believe it was the combination of commercial farmer and environmentalist that makes a modern landowner. The conviction that even nature responds to a helping hand and that, by careful execution, I could create a haven that could be shared by wildlife, farming and men. The will to mould the clay of this little part of the world.

The stream had long been suffering the effects of ruthless dredging by the water authorities, from a time when water was king and the environment a rude word. I took advice on the stream and on my hypothetical lake: water levels and flow, area, positioning and shade. So, when I also invited the officer from the farming and wildlife advisory group to give her opinion of the valley and its potential, I felt I was armed with more than just my own convictions.

Above the flooded meadow was an area of poplars and a disused duck flight pond. The idea of a shallow area next to this as part of a wildlife corridor was her most ardent idea. She was not against a larger lake, but felt a quiet area was essential. The valley as a whole was a revelation to her. Could she return and do a species count? The prospects of expanding the wildlife of the valley had always been here; increasingly I felt a desire to marry them to my own ideas.

The digger driver arrived in late June, just a couple of days before the Royal Show. I took him to the riverbank at the very top of the meadow, still an oozing tidal-like expanse, despite the summer sun.

'Build up a ten-metre platform here', I said, prodding the ground with my stick, 'and then continue it on down to the lasher', pointing to the small waterfall surrounded by willow trees two hundred metres below us.

'You will have to take quite a bit of soil from the meadow to build up this bank, but it should keep the water where it belongs.' We turned to re-cross the meadow,

'Oh yes, don't just leave the holes as ugly and stagnant, landscape them, you know, make a bit of a lake if you like.' He nodded, understanding, and smiled.

The Royal Show started for us on the Saturday when we took up our sheep, and we didn't return until the Thursday.

'The lake is coming well, but we've decided to put in a third island', said my father, upon our return. The next morning, I went to see. The area was of mud but obviously drying fast. The stream, now back in its mill race confines, bubbled happily over the stones and between the thorn-guarded banks.

A handful of holes, as bomb craters, pot-marked the base of the would-be lake, and the banks on the bottom side rose rugged and strong. The digger was rolling the tops of these. As he saw me, the driver jumped down and came over, looking like a wicked schoolboy, but a proud one. He asked what I thought. I looked about me, took in the three islands, the gentle curves of the far bank contrasting with the straight side next to the stream. He had obviously enjoyed himself, freed from the attentions of surveyors and architects, no written measures or levels, with no one to interfere.

'Yes, very good', I said, nodding my approval. He seemed relieved and released into a flood of explanation of what he had done.

'I should have done it this way', he began, and then rushed off into how it had really come together.

Over the next few days, we constructed the inlet and outlet areas. Levels were set purely by eye and when the water was finally released into the shell of drying mud, we waited with excitement and apprehension.

As the water rose, it seemed that we may have made the outlet too high but, as it started to trickle and then gently flow back into the stream below the lasher, it looked about right. I was amazed how clear and serene the water rapidly became. A moorhen skidded across the surface and into the safety of the poplars. Soon there would be more.

The lake had only been there a year but had already merged well into the meadow when the Daniels came to stay. An American couple in their mid-forties with a sixteen-year-old daughter. It was a hot Friday in late July and the thick stone walls of the farmhouse gave a superb cooling effect. We sat around the table taking our customary cup of tea. They had driven down from the north that day and were enjoying the rest, after the heat and dust of the road. Conversation had followed their northern tour and, having arrived at the house, was spreading across the farm. The lake came to the fore.

'Can you swim in the lake?', asked Mrs Daniels, in a bright, hopeful voice. The landing stage had been constructed at the bottom end of the lake with water between ten and fourteen feet deep between it and the first island, some forty yards away.

'Yes', I said, 'although, as the water is constantly flowing through the lake, it will be quite cool'. No matter, the idea had formed and set in an instant. The daughter wanted to swim.

I showed them the way across the old dairy field, over the bridge and up to the lake. The birds had become used to quiet onlookers wanting to share their paradise. The sun glistened on the small ripples as a gentle breeze brought the first hint of dusk. Two ducks circled overhead and a coot called as the girl slipped out of her jeans to reveal her hardly decent bikini. She slid gingerly into the crystal-clear water and swam effortlessly towards the island. A picture of absolute beauty that suddenly made me feel very old.

Above the lake, the river meanders in a chaotic mixture of long arcs and short sharp oxbow wriggles, as if trying to shake off some tormentor. In the valley, dense and rushed, orchids and willow shrub give way to the bleak slopes by Worcester Hill. Worcester Hill, brooding mother-like over the valley and the farm itself, had always been able to mother me too. Its narrow sheep walks tell of so many times; its constant battle of the short suckling clovers against the onset of the thorn; its great appreciation of the seasons. I loved the autumn, with the valley below hung heavy with haw frost or viewed through a veil of mist. I was renewed by the spring, with the greens and blues of the new year talking to the dull rush of the old that led into the high summer, with the wind turning the willow bows inside out, showing leaves in a constant contrast of light and dark. Worcester Hill was a place for all seasons.

I would walk here when I was young, trying to make sense of the changing world. It fell into place then without the need to ask any questions; mystically, as can only be seen and understood through the eyes of a child. Today, with the changes so much greater, I need so much more, but the child's eyes are gone. Yes, I can still relax here as nowhere else and feel a sense of belonging, but the oneness is gone. Now, questions are asked but answers are harder to find.

The steep valley sides that fall away from the barren plateau above face north, south and east, as the river wanders unsteadily below. Each side tells a different story and responds to different moods, seasons and memories. The river near the lake and mill race below the house belong to crayfishing with my grandfather on July afternoons. From my earliest memories, he carried a stick and stooped, eternally lighting his pipe. Crayfish were nocturnal feeders and our daytime outings resulted in only half a dozen or so of the small freshwater lobsters. The nets were made of metal hoops a foot in diameter, filled with netting and weighted in the centre. Strung so they could be lifted horizontally, using a forked stick or an old pitchfork, each net's emergence from the water was a time of great expectations.

As a very small boy, everything was so large and exciting, even the smallest fish sitting back on its tail and waving its claws angrily in the air. The larger fish were taken home triumphantly in a metal bucket, scratching and clawing noisily against the sides, filling a small boy with fear they would escape, which, of course, they never did. Cooked in boiling water, they turned a bright red and would be eaten at tea with plates of fresh, buttered bread and my grandmother's special sponge cake to follow.

As the years passed, crayfishing became an excuse for an all-night party after harvest, and the venue moved upstream to the broad meanders below Worcester Hill. A huge bonfire threw a lively glow across the valley and bursts of sparks high into the night air. The grain trailer had been hastily converted into a bar and cases and crates bounced and clattered precariously as we made our way up the well-worn track that led from the farmhouse and buildings and on, through the middle of the farm. Finally, we would turn, and the valley would open up below us. Dull trees rapidly losing their shape in a duller background. The only sign of life, a faint glow from round the next headland, would break into a sharp spear of light. Around its base, people as shadows would move from barbeque to river and back, breaking the neat circle of seated, silent folk. The sound came as we drew nearer, suddenly rising above the purr of the tractor, making the whole scene immediate and personal. Crayfish were caught and cooked on the edge of the fire, and sausages sizzled in a well-balanced pan. But the feeling was not that of any singular experience, more a general joy in being alive and there. The valley became an amphitheatre and the fire its stage.

They tried to televise it once, to analyse this historic Cotswold custom but, as with all analysis, it became too clinical and showed only as something dead and soulless.

As the late summer mist settled into the valley, the heat of the fire burnt a clearing of visibility where a bee-like energy and urgency was infectious. The noise seemed trapped by the warmth, with the fire, barbeque and bar a constant circuit of strangers sharing loud jokes. Beyond, the raw openness hit me suddenly. It was the place and time for drawing breath, sensing the valley reasserting its dominance and becoming a subservient part of it. The place for one-to-one encounters, quiet words or a peck on the cheek. I wanted to feel the wind in my hair, but the valley was still and heavy, everything looking in on me as I stumbled by.

It was a time for all generations. Great aunt propped against a bale, enjoying the glow, the buzz, the people, and the memories. Young children running excitedly with news of the latest catch, trying to drink drinks they knew they shouldn't have, till they collapsed, curled on a broken bale in the glow and warmth of the fire and drifted into perfect sleep.

In the morning, the bright hope of an autumn day drove away the mist and many of the memories. Buzzards soared above the leftover crayfish and half-eaten sausages. Glasses hidden under bales and litter, weighted by the morning dew, seemed out of place. The bales were loaded and the smoking embers raked, bursting into flames as the trailer clawed its way back up the headland. Nature could emerge again. We had returned the key and, with a heartfelt thank you, I shut the gate and drove back to reality.

The gate is still the same, with the same twist. It still opens the door from reality, with its stormy uncertainty, to something that asks no questions and where I am always a favoured guest. The crayfish are fewer now, a victim of man and time, and with them has gone the excuse for the party. But if I walk around the valley at dusk, or in the morning, I know that it is only me that has really changed. I take a deep breath and think of a poem I wrote in my early teens and which seems more relevant to me now than ever.

> On Worst' Hill's stony brash I walk,
> My childhood friend below.
> I only want to look and talk,
> Do anything but grow.
>
> For now those thoughts so dear to me,
> Already going fast,
> Seem drowned in life's reality,
> How long can I make them last?
>
> Those summer days by the water side,
> A picnic in the grass,
> Seem going like an outward tide,
> How distant they will pass?
>
> I wonder at my childish joy,

Those battles in the hay.
Was I really such a little boy?
Will there be another day?

Those monstrous walls, now small and free,
O'er grown with grass and moss,
Did once divide the world for me
And I marvel at the loss.

But the river still flows on the same,
Her calm tranquillity,
I'll leave the world with all its blame
There'll just be her and me.

5

CHAPTER FIVE

Whenever and however in life you manage to escape the shackles of reality, there is always something to bring you back to earth with a bump. My something is invariably machinery, especially at harvest time.

The barley crop had been steadily ripening in the field; the ears of grain forcing their way skyward, then knuckling over as if exhausted by their efforts, till, finally, the bright greens give way to a sombre brown. It never quite achieves the golden glow of wheat but, however I try to ignore it, to put it off, ripeness always arrives before I am ready. In a dry time on our light brash soil the crop dies as it ripens and its ability to tolerate a spate of wet weather is reduced. The advantage of a fine, dry grain, which is easy to harvest and store, is significant and, as such, timeliness is important.

All this was alive in my mind as I walked the fields on the Sunday evening, flowing my hand through the standing crop, breaking off ears of grain and rubbing them out in the palm of my hand. I looked across the field, watching for green patches or areas where the wind had driven the crop flat on the ground. I bit grains between my teeth, gauging ripeness and moisture. I reached the edge of the field and looked back across it. Yes, it is ripe, the harvest must begin.

Making this mental statement was much easier than putting it into practice. The barn where the grain was to be stored still needed sweeping. The trailer, which would convey the grain from the field, needed its extension sides fitted and, most important, the old combine that had been moved outside at lambing time was rapidly disappearing behind the nettles.

My father, who in retirement had become a self-appointed consultant, had obviously viewed the barley crop with the same conclusions.

'Your crop looks ready; when are you starting harvest?', he said, as he passed me in the yard. This was the time for positive comment. I looked up and took a deep breath, then glanced at my watch.

'Well, I intend to sweep the barn and prepare the trailer this morning, give the combine a once-over this afternoon and start the field after tea.' He looked shocked.

'Don't be ridiculous, you haven't looked at the combine, you don't even know if it will start.' I felt a tug of loyalty to the old machine; now nearly twenty years old and rapidly wearing out, it deserved my support. I tried to speak with utter confidence, to hide the reality that some problem was likely, as if my show of confidence would somehow improve its mechanical condition.

I had no problems sweeping the barn. The broom remained intact and I took this as a show of confidence in me by the infantry of my mechanical army. The trailer came together well, the nuts, bolts and extension sides fitted with the help of some padding and a few sharp blows with a French screwdriver. I enjoyed my lunch. I was on track with the preparation timetable and was preparing myself for the disasters I feared were waiting for me later. I felt rather like a village batsman facing a first-class fast bowler on a poor pitch.

Fatalism hung heavily in the air. I walked around the old combine, pushing away some weeds here, checking a belt there, looking underneath for oil patches in the stony soil. I could delay it no longer. Grasping the handrail, I pulled myself up and into the cab. The oil and water levels were adequate, as was the fuel and, as I turned the key, the ignition light shone brightly. I sighed aloud, the first hurdle was cleared, the battery wasn't flat. My father had been mowing his lawn and was now tending the garden, well within earshot. I pushed the engine warmer button and spoke to the combine.

'Now girl, I stood up for you earlier, I want to see what you can do. You will start.'

I lent on the lever and the starter swung the engine, over and over, faster and faster. It seemed to falter but then fired and opened into a mighty roar, belching black smoke into the cloudless sky. I tapped the steering wheel and breathed again, another hurdle and we were going well. Now for the hydraulics. I flicked the switch with my finger. The groan of long-idle oil forced through long-idle pipes preceded the squeaks, as the front table slowly lifted clear of its blocks. I shut down the engine and toured the combine, greasing here, oiling there; I would have whistled if I could.

Finally, I climbed back into the driver's seat, the fear and trepidation of my earlier visit now replaced with bland confidence. The engine had started well, the thrashing mechanism come to life and I reversed slowly from the nettles. I enjoyed my tea even more than my lunch. As I drove up the track en route to the barley field I was riding into the winner's enclosure on board a hundred-to-one outsider. I opened the engine to thrashing speed and, lowering the header, moved into the crop.

The engine seemed to purr, grateful to be free of the choking nettles. That she was old and needed coaxing made her all the more personal. I talked her round the first circuit and emptied the grain into the trailer. A fair crop of good grain. The next day dawned bright and clear and we, the combine and I, were soon dancing through the field. My brother had bought a bigger and newer combine during the winter and started his field over the hedge. The drought had intervened, stunting the crop and making it difficult to thrash. By the end of the day I had completed most of the field as my father and brother appeared, on their way home.

'This is how your grain should be', my father said, handing my brother a sample from the trailer.

The next day, I finished the crop in good time and noticed my brother's combine standing idle in the middle of the field, clearly receiving mechanical assistance. I was tempted to pull through and offer to help but thought better of it. When I mentioned it to my father later, he smiled.

'I'm glad you didn't, he hasn't forgiven me for showing him your grain yet.'

I smiled too. It was somehow more satisfying to have had such an easy start to harvest because I hadn't deserved it, like edging a four through the slips or shooting a neighbour's pheasant. Yet I knew that the combine was old and could not do many more years. Her replacement would be expensive and the potential yields from this droughted land not good. Should I allow my brother to do my work with his big machine, or should I change my crop to one I could handle with less machinery and less expense? My brother had proved himself to be a far more competent farmer than me and I valued his experience. Another question to answer, but for now I would enjoy the success of the day. I tipped the last load into the barn, picked up a double handful and let the grain flow through my fingers. It was time for a much-needed shower and a well-deserved cup of tea.

With the end of July, came not only harvest on the farm but also school holidays. James returned from his first term away in a very buoyant mood. He had played regularly for the cricket team, made some good friends and boarding school was most definitely to his liking. Vicki, who had found the busy roads on her journey to Oxford every morning and then back at night very tiresome, was already showing signs of wanting to fly the nest.

With the holidays came a different breed of guest - the family. If the eccentricities of nationality are an interesting aside in the operation of Bed and Breakfast, then the attitudes of parents to children and to their behaviour takes it one stage further. Again, it is probably unfair to make generalisations based on nationality but, in the sphere of parents and children, less so than with individuals.

Not only does Ethel, an ageing mother from Boston recovering from her third facelift, say, 'Pass the Preserve, honey', when she wants the marmalade and then spreads it thickly on her fried bread before continuing to eat her bacon and egg; but she has no eyes for Honey Jr. He may be tormenting the cat or spreading butter on his table mat, but he will certainly interrupt his mother at every opportunity.

'We came through Oxford, it was lovely', Ethel would start, then, 'I want more cornflakes!', Junior would interrupt, having spilt enough milk to symbolise war manoeuvres, mostly amphibious. Ethel would not pause, 'those spires are unreal'. So was Honey Senior, blissfully looking into space, somehow switched off from Junior and Ethel. Junior had now discovered the possibilities of his mess and was spreading it with a spoon; meanwhile, Ethel's verbal monologue had reached the Ashmolean.

As far as their doting parents were concerned, this was to be taken as being advanced and grown up; speaking in turn, with natural respect for elders, definitely taboo. To most other people in the vicinity, the word 'foreword' in this context would mean precocious and probably loud. Self-confidence taken to the level of conceit could easily give you a desire to extend the use of corporal punishment and is only prevented by the deep intake of breath and rapid departure. A well-developed sense of humour is rarely adequate.

The Hardings arrived in the mid-afternoon and were looking forward to the four days they had booked with us. Although Americans, they were only travelling from Suffolk where Mr Harding Snr was in the U.S.A.F.

'Hi', said Joe in a deep voice and struggling to lift a heavy case from the back of their large estate car. His fine-cropped hair shone in the morning sun, hiding the increasing grey. His elder son, pale-faced, looked disinterested.

'Here, son', said Joe, passing out a holdall. The son listlessly picked it up. 'This is gonna be a great holiday', continued Joe, oblivious to the lost looks of the rest of the family.

'Jet lag from Suffolk', I whispered to Chris, before stepping forward to help with the luggage. 'This has the makings of a good Chevy Chase film', I added as I passed, case in hand. We had an image of a partially anglified family who wanted a taste of real English Country Life before their tour of duty came to an end and they rushed back to the U.S.A. With a United States air base only a few miles away, many of our friends over the years had been associated with it and we had decided that they fitted into two main categories. There is the American who is convinced that America is the only country in the world worth bothering with, the rest being here for his amusement. He will barely move from the totally self-contained base, except to pick up an English girl or to noisily consume vast amounts of beer in a formerly quiet English pub. Thankfully, there are others. Couples or families who may have had regrets when first posted here, but who decided to make the most of the country while they were. Often dynamic, they proudly retained their American identity but were open to tasting the British culture at every opportunity.

'Bob, come on over, bring Chris, we're having a barbecue', shouted Stu, over the overgrown wall that separated the cottage they were renting from our neglected back garden. The evening was cool, it was still early June, but Stu skipped about in his light shorts and vivid shirt preparing a delicious feast of meats, sweets and savouries. Beth flowed gracefully to and fro' with salads, dips and various breads, all prepared in what must have been a day-long exercise.

'Come on Bob, you haven't tried this sauce, I learnt the recipe from my grandmother.' Beth cooked at the local pub and Stu, who became a pretty good darts player, served there. Vivid memories of a bright, skin-tight purple tee shirt that followed the flowing contours of his over-weight body jab in my mind. And there were others.

Joan and Alfred moved into the small keeper's cottage in the large expanse of woodland not two miles to the west of us. Their family grown up and flown to the far corners of the world, they had entered their second childhood. The house became an anachronism of genuine English antiques purchased by Joan on her frequent forays to the salerooms, and long delicate curtains sent direct from the U.S., lined throughout in chamois leather to keep out the cold. Those same curtains now adorn our long Sitting Room, purchased from Joan and Alfred when they finally returned home - an ongoing reminder of a great friendship.

One summer evening we had been invited to visit for supper. They were of my parents' generation, whilst we were newly married and childless. Among the collection of antiques was a beautifully decorated chamber pot, which lived on the broad windowsill in the corner. My father, very at home and relaxed in their company, felt able to exercise his practical humour. Quietly picking up the pot, he poured enough of his drink into it to be effective and slid it behind the sofa. The next day Joan was on the phone. 'You didn't!', she began...

Subconsciously, I had hoped the Hardings would be another Joan and Alfred. Dad turned out to be dominant and domineering in everything except parental control. Mum was plain, quiet and totally ineffectual. The boys, of which there were two, had likeable characters, but just when natural discretion and consideration should take them away or shut them up, they would take on a determination based on the blitzkrieg principal. Initially, we encouraged our children to show them around and generally entertain them. Vicki soon dug in her heels and it was left to James. For his tender years, James has a very gregarious nature and willingness to put himself out for others. But even he soon took defensive action.

'I want to see the sheep', said one of the boys in a loud voice, as he entered the kitchen. 'Where is James? I want to see the sheep.'

Chris and I knew that James had taken refuge in his bedroom after a very taxing day.

'James is busy, you can see the sheep later', I said, and carried on with the breakfast.

'I want to see them now, where is James?'

I repeated myself.

'Is he in his room? I'll get him', and the boy was gone.

'No', Chris shouted to the dust trail, 'he is busy and so are we, go and play with your brother!'

We took deep breaths and thought about heads and walls.

At moments like this the parents would be nowhere to be seen. To them, a holiday on a farm meant freedom in every aspect of the word. I thought of suggesting the boys visit the lake, but could picture them rushing up to the commune of half-grown geese and the reaction of the goslings' highly protective parents. I wiped the smile from my face and tried to replace it with benevolence. They were the longest four days of the summer and I was torn between finding essential work at the far end of the farm and protecting my family from this mindless onslaught. As they left, they mentioned coming again next year and I made a mental note that we would certainly be full.

European children, especially French and Germans, have an amazing grasp of the English language. Their natural initial shyness may be due to their undeserved lack of confidence in the language, rather than any undue respect for strangers, but develops after the ice-breaking stage into a quiet dignity.

One busy Saturday, early in the summer holidays, we had filled every room and started one of the saddest parts of Bed and Breakfast, turning people away. It is very easy to make yourself ill by totting up the loss from the three couples who wanted to stay for several days, that you have just sent up the road. You have to become a fatalist and walk away with a shrug of the shoulders, even though your subconscious will be working overtime along the lines of putting bunks into stables or tents in the orchard.

'Have you any room?', asked Kurt in his flat but courteous German English. I was about to go through the 'we are full' routine when three of the most engaging faces I had seen all summer appeared hopefully behind him, filling the doorway with their smiles.

'Come in, I'll see what I can do.'

'What are you doing?' my head said to my heart, looking down in disbelief. 'You know we're full, just say it, WE ARE FULL.' I saw my hand reach out to the diary and open it at today. 'I told you so,' my head interjected: 'WE ARE FULL'. Ideas started to reach my brain. If we could persuade two of them to use the folding double bed in the little sitting room, the other two could use the room in the attic. My brain tried to resist this message but already my voice was speaking, heads were nodding and leggy females were moving off to inspect the beds.

Five minutes later, I entered their names in the diary as the kettle began to boil for their cup of tea. Fantasies filled my heart, of warm, thankful faces cradling their steaming cups, of those bewitching deep brown eyes, of telling my head that it would not always win - and all in the delusion that we only do it for the money.

The lane to the farmhouse, which also serves three more houses beyond, is only one car wide, but this did not stop the large Citroen drawing up in the middle. The father came to the door, leaving a heaving mass of humanity inside. The mother quickly followed, driven by curiosity or desire to escape, perhaps both. We were going through the routine of saying we were full and trying to suggest alternatives, at what was now a very late stage in the evening, when our conversation was halted. The four children had escaped from the car and, as the last one had closed the door, the self-locking mechanism of the advanced Citroen had leapt into action. Considering the apparent ease with which many juveniles seem to be able to break into any car with nothing more than a toothpick, the sight, three hours later, of respected experts with long faces was not amusing.

'But Roger, you are a senior policeman, you must know how to break in.'

Roger's look told me that he considered himself one of the modern pen-pushing policeman, no P.C. Plod from the beat here.

'Do you have a handbook?', I said slowly to the father. He glanced at the car and smiled. It had rapidly become evident that we had a rare combination in our midst, a French family without a word of English between them. My gesticulations merged with rustic pidgin English. Chris laughed. The situation had all the ingredients for good old farce. A policeman who knew nothing about breaking in; a touring family who could not be understood; an access road that was totally blocked and a hostess overcome with the hilarity of her husband's attempts to make any sense. Fatigue had the final say.

'I'm sure we can all fit in somehow', Chris said, more with desperate hope than thought-out reason, as she gestured for everyone to follow her towards the house.

It was finally agreed that, short of breaking a window, nothing could be done about the car till morning. We all turned our attention to the logistics of sleeping. Fortunately, the children were quite young and so tired that they would have slept anywhere. But where to put six people? We finally decided to give them our bedroom, which, with the old bunks that were there more for storage than use and a mattress on the floor, found room for them all to find rest. We moved to the little sitting room downstairs and folded out the sofa bed. This definitely qualified as an ultra-emergency.

There is something very cosy in a home full of people, especially when you think that someday you may be broken down abroad and need a mattress for the night. The morning dawned and, with it, the problem of the Citroen.

'Typical French', I yawned to Chris, as I rolled over in our temporary bed. 'Anyone else would make a car you could get into in five minutes.'

'You can sort out the car while I see if I have enough bacon for breakfast', said Chris. I thought of offering to sort out the bacon problem, it certainly seemed the lesser of the two evils.

We had already invited the neighbours, who could not use the lane, to go out through the farmyard. The A.A. and police having failed, the Citroen dealer was called and finally succeeded. He left with glowing pride in the safety of the Citroen when left unattended, something not shared by the French family. They may have been of few words, but their faces were truly thankful as they left on the next stage of their adventure.

One of the delights of families coming during the holidays is the chance it gives our own children to meet boys and girls of the same age from different countries and with different customs. James and Vicki might not always use the word 'delightful', but it is all part of growing up and finding their feet.

The holidays were in full swing when the Farrant family arrived from France with their sons, Philippe and Peter. The boys were very French, with the makings of handsome young men. At eight, Philippe was the same age as Vicki, who, being blonde, tall and attractive, caused immediate interest. The saga that developed over the next three days varies with the teller, perhaps because I can see the young boys' point of view and because fourteen years of marriage has made me aware that few things girls do are actually by chance.

It will be agreed that Philippe developed a soft spot for Vicki, which resulted in him following her around the house like a lost sheep.

'How will I know when I am in love?', Philippe asked his brother.

'When you are in love, you can think of nothing else', replied the brother, with the utter confidence borne of eleven years' experience.

'Then I am definitely in love', said Philippe, with a glazed look adding to the already sleepy appearance.

Now it is here that accounts vary. The girls in the house claim total innocence in the matter, they offered no encouragement and, in fact, tried to keep away. It is strange, I feel, that whenever Philippe showed signs of returning to the real world, Vicki would appear around the door, turn away and then, with a barely-turned head, give a flash of her eyes and semi-smile before disappearing again. The boy would melt as butter and the circle would rotate once more, like a cat with a mouse, I thought, and smiled to myself. Growing up could be very painful and, of course, the girls were totally innocent in every way.

By the summer, we were getting a fair impression of the Bed and Breakfast potential. The lake still showed its youth, but here too the future was appearing, with small rushes pushing through the mud, sticklebacks in big shoals and an increasing number of water birds using it. Several ducks and two pairs of Canada Geese had moved in during mating time and, although only the geese brought off young, the omens were good. The grassy banks running down to the lake had showed a wealth of wild clovers in the early summer, but were now turned a brittle brown that crunched under your feet in the warmth of the afternoon. The top land grew barley or short-term grassland. The former looked well after the early spring rains, but the latter was struggling to maintain the sheep in these dry times.

The old-fashioned sainfoin crop, deep-rooted and draught resistant, had been suggested as an alternative, an insurance. I would look into it. August, with the children both home and the door thrown open, was the most expansive month. The long days and warm nights seemed to gel with never-ending activity. At times, the hectic daylight hours disguised my utter exhaustion. As I lay in bed, cursing the heat and the airless night that denied me rest, I tried to draw a perspective of the year. But instead of rational comparison, all I saw was a red blur and being dragged below the water by a heavy, lead weight.

The least-used electrical appliance during August is the television, which is probably why I remember the German couple so well. Their English was unusually bad and it had taken some time to realise that they wanted to watch the final instalment of a romantic mini-series that had been running for several nights.

As the programme approached its sad climax, the room was in silence. Vicki, renowned for her ability to really live these emotional sequences, rose from the sofa and collected the box of paper tissues from the kitchen. She walked round the entire company, handing them out and saying, 'One for you, one for you ...' Everyone smiled through watery eyes and broke into gentle, subdued laughter.

The girl, as beautiful as her English was bad, had been distinctly pregnant when she visited us in the August and when we received a Christmas card from her and her young husband that December, we assumed it would mention the baby too. Chris sat very still at the breakfast room table, at the end, as she does, in her favourite wing chair. Her head had been bent forward as she read, and it seemed to remain there for an eternity. Finally, she looked up, card in one hand and short note in the other, with tears welling in her eyes. They had lost the baby. We pictured the scene in August, those mock tears around the television when we all knew it was make-believe. This time it was real and, although we had known them for only one night, we needed more than Vicki's tissues to make us laugh.

~~~~~~~~~~~~~~~~~~~~~

Many guests don't ask if we have cows or pigs, sheep or goats. They want to know if we have horses.

'Are they yours?', asked the young girl, looking out of the Breakfast Room window at the horses grazing in the paddock below. Her parents were still discussing whether to stop or whether to travel a little further and save time the next day.

'I will be with the horses', called the girl, as she received Chris's approving nod and was gone across the drive. Her parents knew when they were beaten. 'We'll take the family room', they said, smiling a smile of approved resignation.

My grandfather was from a keen hunting family and, standing at no more than 5' 2' tall, was designed to sit on a horse. My mother was not at all interested and when I showed no interest either, it was a great disappointment to him. Chris had ridden competitively and well, until injury forced her to take a more gentle approach. She talked me into the saddle soon after we were married, and I found it far less terrifying than I had expected. I never became keen but could hack along without feeling totally hard done by.

James's initial interest at the age of three led to Bonnie coming on loan. A black Shetland, she soon showed to have fewer vices than her reputation had stated. Intelligent and brave, she proved the ideal first pony for a young boy, who quickly showed a genuine, if chauvinistic liking for the sport. He went the way of most farmer's son riders and attended the pony club camp. He was tested on the parts of his horse and demonstrated a fair knowledge, but when the questioning switched to his tack and its care, his ability to answer deserted him.

'Don't you look after your own tack?', asked the matronly figure, with growing exasperation.

James thought for a moment, 'Well, you see, the girls so enjoy doing it that it would be cruel of me not to let them.'

He passed the test. Vicki also learnt to ride on Bonny and became a very correct and proficient rider. As with many young people, the distractions of life soon led to a decline in riding, but their basic knowledge was such that they would always be able to return to it if the desire or need arose.

Bonny was put in foal to a welsh stallion with the reputation for throwing large foals, and the time for the birth arrived. We had booked a holiday in Cornwall for the following week and, when departure day arrived and there was still no foal, we left mum-to-be in the care of my father. A main topic of conversation became the name for the foal.

'If it goes fast, we will call it 'Gallop' and if it doesn't, we will call it 'Slowly", said Vicki.

We phoned home every night and, for once, Vicki would be first through the door, buzzing infectively. For three days, nothing happened and we thought we might even make it back for the birth. Finally, on the fourth day, the much-anticipated news came.

'It's a light bay', my father began his telephonic conversation.

'How big is it, how fast does it go?', bounced Vicki, in a blaze of excitement.

'It was born last night and was galloping with the rest at first light.'

'Does it gallop quickly?', asked Vicki, with sudden seriousness. She went quiet, waiting; the name would depend on this crucial answer.

'It gallops very quickly', replied my father, after a deliberate, teasing delay.

'Then we will call it Gallop.' This was not a request - Vicki was not into requests - it was a decision and a decision that had been made. So, we had a light bay colt called Gallop. He grew into a fine, bright bay gelding, which broke with incredible ease. Late one evening, James announced he would like to go hunting on Gallop. Now five years old and well-schooled, Gallop had never hunted and James had not ridden for a year. Yet Chris was keen to encourage her son; Gallop was pronounced ready and, although Chris was off riding following a leg injury, Eleanor, who had become a very proficient rider, would be able to go too.

'What a good idea', said Chris, checking to see where the hunt met next day. 'I will pay you three pounds for every jump you take.'

Chris left early with James and Eleanor, climbing into the old lorry and heading to the meet, high in the Cotswolds. The going was good, the sun was shining and, having seen him off, Chris settled back in the lorry to wait for the return of her son. She felt sure it would not be a long wait but, as time passed, she became anxious. One of the hunt masters rode by and he promised to look out for him.

'I've seen him and he's going well', he shouted, as they passed sometime later.

The sun was dropping in the sky and anxiety was growing into worry, when the same master came slowly up the road, homeward bound.

'They're about eight miles out and going away; I just followed your son over a stone wall.'

Christ felt relieved and very proud. Both riders and horses returned safely, though Chris was never foolhardy enough to offer the same inducement again. Vicki also loved hunting, but her great joy was the meet, the people, the hounds, the atmosphere, but especially the stirrup cup. The stirrup cup is the drink offered by the host of the meet to the riders, usually sherry or port. Vicki's taste was for the port. She always looked incredibly smart and rode with great pride and style, though she was not one for long days and fast gallops. Soon after the meet, she would smile a deep, rosy smile and say, 'I'm tired, I think I will go home.'

As the children grew up, both Bonny and Gallop were broken to harness and exercised in an old Governess cart. We had great fun travelling the local lanes on summer afternoons, the guests loved it and more than once it proved its practical worth.

One bright Sunday, our Rector, Leonard, had joined us for a post-church drink. The drink had drifted into lunch and the post-lunch rest was suddenly interrupted.

'What time is it?', demanded Leonard, sitting up in his chair.

'Half-past five', said Chris, 'why?'

'I've got to take Evensong at Kiddington at six', he replied, still not fully recovered from his deep sleep.

Although by no means under the influence, we had all drunk too well to drive, but Chris soon had the answer.

'Get your things together, I will pick you up in five minutes.'

Gallop was soon tacked up and, with Leonard and Chris safely aboard, the three-mile journey was completed in time. Whilst the service went on inside the church, Gallop happily grazed in the churchyard, building up his strength for the return trip, just as would have been done a hundred years before.

Bonny went away to teach another young child to ride and Gallop now competes in national harness events. Although I would never claim to ride - I merely sit on a horse - I feel the experience our children have gained from riding has given them not only confidence, but a skill that will be with them all their lives. We have fewer horses now, but when our guests walk along the row of interested heads, rubbing noses and cooing, I think to myself, 'You know only the half of it.'

6

CHAPTER SIX

It is so easy to think of August as being the time of summer holidays, of children, of harvest and of hot, dusty days. A time when there is no time. The days seem so long and the nights hot and sleepless. At least, these are what I remember as I place the month in the order of things, when summer has reached its peak and is ready to slip gently into autumn. Sometimes, when the storm that has threatened for days actually breaks and swills away the dust from my mind, as well as the air, I can look back at my mistakes and regrets and see amongst them the times that have made me smile. I see the people who punctuated the daily run; people like Naoki, who had come for the British Grand Prix at Silverstone.

'I have flown in just for the race', he began in short, sharp, abbreviated English. 'Tomorrow they practise and on Sunday is the race.'

His arms opened wide and his face grinned accordingly, teeth gleaming, white and even. His enthusiasm infectious, confidence tempered with consideration. Very much Japanese and very much a bachelor, his pride and desire to show respect for his hosts was evident. He entered the house one afternoon as Chris was clearing the Breakfast Room. It was hot and, by chance, Chris was barefoot. He put his bags in the hall and came through for a cup of tea. He looked about, taking in the furniture, the high ceiling and old flagstone floor. Suddenly his steadily relaxing glow turned to horror.

'I am sorry, I am sorry', he stammered. He rose, bowing, from the table and reversed towards the door. His face had become tortured with apologies as he continued to bow till he disappeared out of the front door. After a few seconds he reappeared, minus shoes. He had confused the Japanese custom of removing shoes before entering a home with Chris's shoeless state. Our respect for his intentions only just prevented us from laughing and, as he realised his error, he joined us in an amused smile.

At about the same time, Liz and Tony came to stay whilst attending a friend's wedding. They arrived during the morning, hot and rushed after their trip from London, but reappeared later, pristine and ready. Liz was naturally beautiful, with a confident, relaxed air about her. Tony found it more difficult to relax. He was obviously concerned about his family connections, his appearance, his image. They left to join a party for a pub meal, with us reassuring them that the house would be open for their late return.

We were watching a late-night film when we heard them come back. The car drew up carefully, as if itself trying to be especially quiet, not to disturb. For an eternity, there was total peace. The car had come to a halt and the engine stopped, but no opening of doors heralded their next movement. Finally, the sound returned, muffled voices and scuffing feet on the gravel. The front door opened with an exaggerated flourish, banging against the stop and followed by muted but clear curses. The hallway was narrow and flanked by a cabinet on one side and hanging coats on the other. Wide enough for passage normally in single file, but obviously a problem now. I wanted to help, could picture tall, well-built Tony in his well-below par condition, and the diminutive Liz trying to coax him to the relative safety of their room before their reputation disappeared with their discovery. Tony needed a shoulder for support as well as a helmsman for direction, but the width of the hall made this nigh impossible. I could picture him bouncing from cabinet to coat, struggling for balance, looking for a strange room without the advantage of the automatic pilot that would help him in a house he knew well. They reached the bottom of the stairs, Liz encouraging in low but determined whispers.

Directly opposite the bottom of the stairs is the door from the hall to the sitting room, where we sat, rapidly losing the plot of the film as the more local drama unfolded. They seemed to be doing well, to have climbed several stairs, when Tony lost his footing, stumbled back and landed with a crash against the door. After a short silence, they tried again, Liz's whispers becoming louder, but still determined rather than desperate. Chris and I looked at each other, should we offer to help, for Liz's benefit as well as that of the fabric of the house? Not yet, Liz had done so well, we must give her every chance to save their dignity.

After three attempts they achieved the first bend of stairs and, as their voices and sounds disappeared into the night, we knew they had made it. In the morning they were down for breakfast, as promised, Tony amazingly full of himself and Liz with brave face and barely concealed anger. I tried not to tell myself that she was too good for him but somehow I wouldn't listen.

~~~~~~~~~~~~~~~~~~~~~

Every two years, a national sheep event is held at Malvern in Worcestershire. Although predictable in its content, it gives me a chance to meet old friends and potential customers, as well as keep up with any new ideas that are trying to become fashionable. This year's event was to be different, as a group of Dutch farmers were visiting our farm en route to Malvern. Despite our through-put of foreign visitors, my ability to speak or even understand foreign languages has not improved at all. As I waited for the bus, I remembered my vain attempts to communicate with Dutch sheep breeders while visiting Holland several years before. In the event, visual gesticulation proved an ample language between one sheep breeder and another and, needless to say, their English was more than adequate.

We drove through a field of ewes recently separated from their lambs, about which the visitors made polite comments. It was clear, though, that these sheep, which were based on French breeding, were not their type. We specialise in the Texel breed. Over the years, the French Texels have grown larger and longer, while the Dutch have become smaller, shorter and meatier, to the extent that in many ways they now appear as two separate breeds.

Later, we drove through a field of rams, mainly young animals being reared on for sale as stock sires in the autumn. Amongst them were our own stock rams, one of which, known as 'Shah', was meatier than the rest and, I suspected, more appealing to the visitors. I walked through the sheep till I passed Shah, when I reached out, caught him, and invited their opinions. Their attitudes immediately changed, their sign language demonstrating where their speech couldn't, their admiration obvious and genuine.

One of them spoke better English than the rest and asked about Shah's breeding.

'He must be Dutch', he said, with complete confidence. When told he was of French origin he was amazed and rapidly transmitted this amazement to the rest of his party. They were not to be beaten.

'From which French flock does he come?', he asked, as Shah became totally encircled by Dutchmen anxious to handle him and confirm their visual impression. I told them that his ancestors came from the flock of

Jacque Pelzer in the Ardennes. A broad smile spread across the translator's face.

'Monsieur Pelzer, ah yes, he uses a Dutch ram every four years, that is where his quality must come from.' The fact that, by this reckoning, Shah could have only one or two percent Dutch blood was irrelevant; they had settled in their minds that Dutch was still best and were happy. I waved away offers to load Shah into the boot of the bus and suggested they buy some semen in future years. They left for Malvern, grateful for my tour and convinced that my best sheep was so because of his Dutch connections, however dilute.

Chris, the sheep breeder friend from Norfolk and much-heckled cricketer, arrived during the evening, ready for an early start the next day. We were travelling together to Malvern to enjoy the show and study the carcase competition. Texels are the ultimate carcase breed and the competition between breeders to produce better-shaped animals is intense. In the early years, when I was trying to establish my Texels as superior sheep before commercial farmers, who were used to traditional breeds, the carcase competitions were important events. As I toured the show, I thought of the competitions we had entered and the championships we had won.

The Bath and West show at Shepton Mallett became an early favourite. At first, there would be few entries with Texel-sired lambs, and such was the improvement that a rosette was almost assured. The main problem was weight. The limits for each class were very close and no swapping between classes was allowed. I arrived late and was weary after the three-hour bank holiday drive. The lambs were missing their mothers and feeling the heat too.

'They're not heavy enough', I heard the steward say, as he wrote the weight on his list. There was no sadness, certainly no apology for rendering my journey wasted. Well, not quite wasted, the lighter group of lambs were just in the weight band, but I still felt annoyed. The joy at having arrived turned into a dry anger.

'But they were right at home, it's only the journey and the heat.' The steward was unmoved.

'They can go with the rest and you will receive the basic price, but they cannot be shown.' The basic price at that time of year was very poor and I knew my lambs to be worth much more. It was the final straw.

'They certainly won't go with the rest, I will take them home and show them elsewhere, where they will be appreciated.' My comment was water off a duck's back to this bureaucratic oaf.

'Why don't you work for the civil service?' I thought, 'or perhaps you already do'. Soon, however, the consequences of my verbal anger came to mind. The trailer that had carried the lambs down had been borrowed by a friend and would not be back till tomorrow. Tomorrow, the day when Chris and I were due at a friend's wedding and for which Chris had been cleaning the car, inside and out, for days.

The fish and chip shop was half-way home, and served to remind me that I had missed lunch. I can still remember those three angelic, white faces looking at me through the rear window and the surprise on the counter girl's face as I turned and said to them,

'I know you don't want vinegar, now sit down.'

The girl's expression as they replied with a gentle bleat made me smile, but both melt into insignificance when compared with the look on Chris's face when she saw the car on my arrival home, and the back seat, where my three woolly friends had enjoyed the journey.

Our first attempt at the Royal Show came readily to mind. We had very few Texel sheep in those early days and were going to find it difficult to produce a pair of carcases for the event. It is accepted that for a matching pair of live lambs to become a matching pair of carcases, they must be of the same breed, the same sex and weigh the same. Our only vaguely suitable lambs were of different cross-breeds, opposite sex and, ten days before the show, of significantly different weights.

'Are you sure it only weighs 32 kilos?', I asked, as the lamb I had expected to be the match for my earlier selection stood on the scales. The dial moved chaotically, as the lamb moved backwards and forwards before taking breaths, stationary just long enough for us to see: 32 kilos. The fine, twin-reared, threequarter bred Texel lamb in front of me suddenly looked very different to the Texel half-bred, single-reared lamb we had weighed earlier. The eight-kilo difference in weight was testimony to that. By controlled diet we narrowed the weight difference, but the sex and breed variation still seemed an insurmountable problem.

We were breaking every convention of carcass showing and, when we were told only the best would be exhibited, we thought our show was over. To find that we had been awarded third prize was all the more satisfying because it was undeserved; like a small boy climbing a wall to get a neighbour's apples. In later years, we achieved first prize, but the satisfaction I felt then was far less than for this early lesser award.

Some may find it difficult, even offensive, to consider live animals as lumps of meat, yet people enjoy eating meat and especially good meat. I hope I am a sufficient realist to know that good meat doesn't just happen, but follows careful breeding and a contented, stress-free life. If I have produced a fine animal, which enjoys such a contented life and which has been so produced purely to become succulent meat, I consider that better than to have produced no animal, no life, no meat at all.

Our return from Malvern brought us home by early evening and to a worried father. The existing conservative member of parliament had announced he was not going to stand at the next election and the new prospective candidate for the area had just been selected. He was doing the rounds of the constituency, introducing himself to loyal followers and hoping for support. He was due in the village tonight. My father was concerned that the turn-out would be poor and dragooned us into attendance. Norfolk Chris was single and, as such, had only brought one shirt. I loaned him one, which happened to be blue, and a tie, which was a darker blue.

My wife and I accompanied our guest into the grounds of Wootton Place, the grand former rectory, where the introduction was to take place. The prospective candidate had not arrived and the appearance of this handsome, suitably dressed stranger led to immediate confusion.

'Are you our prospective candidate?', asked the aging hostess, as she met Chris approaching the front entrance. Chris has always been able to rise to the occasion and seized his chance.

'Would you like me to be, madam? Then I will', shaking her hand in his confident, positive way.

During the next half-hour and until the arrival of the real candidate, Chris gloried in his new vocation. On the lawn, a very staunch girl, both physically and politically, was trying to play croquet. Chris rushed to her aid. As she stood, mallet gently swinging backwards and forwards between widely-spread legs, he put his arms around her from behind and said, in a broad Norfolk accent,

'No, my dear, your stance is all wrong.'

He made a rapid departure as the real politician arrived but, in many ways, after the tut-tutting had finished, there was a certain regret in the air, though few would openly admit it.

~~~~~~~~~~~~~~~~~~~~~~

So much has happened over the fourteen years since our first Texel purchase. The flock has developed from the few purchased at Lanark on a wet September day and now numbers over a hundred females. We have made so many friends and are, in many ways, different people. Although the farm is changing now, developing from that raw idea, hatched on a cold February morning, the seed for where we are today may well have been sown those fourteen years ago. I had first seen Texels whilst on a highly alcoholic Easter study tour during my time at the Royal Agricultural College. I had been impressed by their shape and ability to produce lean meat, increasingly an important consideration.

Several years later, I noticed an advert for the second annual sale of Texels at Lanark. Chris and I had been married for less than a year and the novelty and madness of life still carried all before it.

'Let's go and have a look, see what they're really like.' My father thought that this mad idea to travel over seven hundred miles just to have a look would wear off. The motorway network was far from complete and the journey much longer than it seems today. He was genuinely surprised that the idea did not, in fact, wear off and that we were actually determined to go. He dropped in for a coffee on the Wednesday morning, nervous, beating about the bush before coming to the point.

'If you're going all that way, you had better take the cheque book.' My eyes lit up. He continued, 'I wouldn't buy any females, but a ram to try on some of the old ewes would be worthwhile.'

I had been thrown by this statement, not only of generosity, but more of confidence in me. In those days, a good traditional ram could be bought for fifty pounds; I knew a Texel would be much more and thought I should prepare him for it.

'A ram will cost three figures, you know', I said, anxious not to commit myself to any specific figure.

'Oh yes, you will need two hundred for a fair sheep, I'm sure', he said, in a way that implied I could go to three hundred.

Looking back, our plans for attending the sale were insane. We had arranged to join some friends on the Wednesday evening for supper, then drive up overnight to Lanark, buy a ram, and return in time for a cray fishing party in the evening. It seemed fated from the outset. Our friends had written the wrong day in their diary and were expecting us the next night. We had a quick drink and left them with their embarrassment, stopping off for a bag of fish and chips as we tried to benefit from an earlier journey.

The weather turned nasty as we crossed the border, the old Renault car rocked by gusts of horizontal rain driving across the road. We pulled into a lay-by five miles short of Lanark but, although we were both desperately tired, the noise of the rain and violent rocking of the car made sea sickness more likely than sleep. We limped into a Lanark hotel in the morning, freshened up, and were brought back to humanity by a fine Scottish breakfast.

For several years I had carried the responsibility for buying all the calves for our beef enterprise, competing with dealers for the few good specimens in the local market, yet I felt totally unprepared for the experience that awaited me. My knowledge of Texels was limited to a drunken haze and exhibition animals at shows, neither relevant to today. I could check the rams on offer for correctness, straight legs and sound mouths, but my knowledge of breed points was a thing for the future.

'I like lot 99', I uttered, pointing my stick at the young ram at the back of the pen. Then, hanging the stick on the rail, I opened the gate and went in. I stood back at first, comparing its size and length to the five contemporaries that were moving about, doing their best to obscure my view.

'It's longer than some, but is it wide enough.' Trapping it in the corner, I held it with my left hand under its mouth, my right hand behind, preventing it from reversing until it settled. Born in February or March, these lambs had grown a fair bit of wool by September. It was necessary to feel through the wool to ensure the body beneath carried the same qualities.

'I think I prefer lot 101', said Chris, after several minutes' silence. I released 99. The two stood side by side, in fact, all six now stood in a line, looking away, and with identification hanging from their necks, all unidentifiable.

'Which is yours?', said Chris, entering the pen.

I hesitated. 'The one on the right.'

'No', she went on, 'that's mine.' Stretching forward, she checked his number.

'Well?', I asked, after her seemingly unnecessary delay.

'It's lot 100', she said, before breaking into barely controlled laughter, which left those in the next pen wanting to share the joke. I could pick out the best animals, but so could everyone else and their cheque book was likely to be bigger than mine.

My confused mind hit further bewilderment as the auctioneer began to speak. I could not understand a word he was saying - was it thirty, or fifty or five hundred. This could be drastic. I settled back, hoping time would help decipher this Celtic code. We had marked several animals in the catalogue and, as they continued to make well over our price, I thought we would be travelling home empty handed.

'Dneister' walked slowly into the ring and looked about. Not a big ram, but correct and definitely masculine. He was not one we had marked, but we liked him. We looked at each other, Chris and I, and agreed without speaking. The bidding rose and reached my limit. Just one more, I thought, and bid again. I waited as the auctioneer tried to prise another bid out of our competitor.

An eternity passed and I dared not look, until the vacuum was broken by a loud crack of hammer on wood and a young clerk asked for my name. We were pleased with our purchase, my head light and euphoric. I found a farmer from just four miles up the road from home, who had also ventured north and bought a ram. His trailer was fine for two sheep and the problems of transport in the rear compartment of the car were avoided. We could not have known how fortunate that was for, just twenty miles down the road, the engine uttered a terrifying, fatalistic cry and died, the car coasting to a halt on an incline adjacent to the now famous town of Lockerbie.

The local garage rapidly diagnosed that a new engine was needed and offered to put the job in hand. We thanked them, but declined and summoned the AA rescue service. That the journey home contained three breakdown lorries breaking down and covered a time span of seventeen and a half hours, brings back too many painful memories for me to want to recount it in detail. That we finally arrived home to assurances that we had missed a superb party only added to the injury.

But Dneister met with approval, enjoyed his selected females and produced some outstanding offspring, whose descendants are still with us today. He lived for many years and, as with many of the good things in life, was perhaps only fully appreciated after his death.

With his travelling companion now six miles up the road, he was the first of his breed in the county. The local radio correspondent arrived the next day; agriculturally this was hot news.

'Now, what breed is it?', he began. 'Is it Taxel?'

I have often wondered how reporters who, by their trade, should know a little about a great many topics, invariably prove they know absolutely nothing about anything as soon as they open their mouths.

'No, it's Texel, spelt Texel, from an island of the same name off the north coast of Holland.'

I had only owned Dneister for a day, but my description of the breed, its history and its attributes already had the feel of a lifetime's repetition. A young, hungry-looking man walked backwards and forwards trying to make the ram interested in having his photo taken. However, many hours of sale preparation and procedure, followed by a long journey, had left the ram convinced that he only wanted to sit and chew. His experiences of the last two days must have convinced him that all men were mad. He finally rose to his feet, the man took his chance - 'click' - and bolted for his car, anxious to return to the sanity of pretty babies and ugly brides.

The man from the paper arrived next. 'Has the photographer been, did he get what he wanted?' It was easier just to say 'Yes'. Within a week, everyone seemed to know about Dneister, who, oblivious to his new stardom, was more interested in eating grass or finding a few females.

My clearest memory is of him grazing the paddock below the house, his favourite place, and of wanting to move him elsewhere. He was a very passive animal to everyone except my father, to whom he had taken a dislike and at whom he would charge at any pretext. We found the easiest way to move Dneister from his favourite field was for my father to enter it by the gate through which we wanted the ram to leave. The ram would then chase him out and we could close the gate. On this particular day, my father had foolishly ventured further into the field and Dneister was feeling especially fit. He caught my father three times before he was lured through the gate, much to everyone's amusement and my father's painful annoyance.

The next year, we added to our single ram, two pure-bred females, imported directly from France. The breed was rapidly gaining in popularity, our enthusiasm was growing and when, the next year, the best of our two ewes was found dead in the field, I felt angry and depressed. I wanted more females and females that would give me the chance to expand quickly. But all the best ewes were being kept by their breeders, only the poor or problem sheep finding their way to the sales.

Eventually, I found a breeder with sheep from the first importation, who had been offered the chance to buy his farm and wanted to raise some money. Chris and I travelled up to Scotland to see his flock; eleven ewes and a young lamb. The rest of the lamb crop were to be sold at the Lanark sale, but he was willing to sell the ewes privately if I bought them all. He stated a price and I made him an offer. He invited us to stay the night while we discussed the difference. The price was agreed in the morning and when, a week later, these sheep ran out of the lorry and on to Manor Farm, I felt a sheep breeder at last. I had a flock, something to work with and build on. I was a happy man.

From such beginnings, the Wootton flock of Texels evolved. Few stars but enough prize winners to gain us respect. I had evolved a true type, with which I was pleased. I hoped our customers were too. What has all this to do with today, with our present larger flock and aspirations for the future? Not only does it show the roots from which this living entity called a 'pedigree flock' has grown, but it helps explain my joy at being asked to judge two shows at the end of August, just before our annual pilgrimage to Lanark.

The first was at Wilton, the famous sheep fair in Hampshire. The classes were not large and were drawn from local breeders. The atmosphere was friendly, the competition being more with other breeds than with each other.

'There are not many round the Suffolk ring', I noted to Chris, as we passed down the main access track and turned right up the Texel lines. I felt strange in my suit and tie, strange to have no sheep of my own. After selling here for several years, I knew all the faces, yet somehow they looked different today. Instead of being one of them, I was their judge. They smiled their 'Hello Bob, morning Chris' as we passed.

'They won't all feel so happy when I've finished', I whispered to Chris. 'There can only be one winner.' Inside, I felt as a player in a game of charades, all procedure and manners, but none of it quite real and none of it relaxed.

The show field had appreciated some late rain after a dry spring and the grass had grown well in recent weeks. I was shown the ring where the grass stood over a foot high. The organisers looked embarrassed; how could sheep be judged when their legs would be barely visible? I summoned all the sheep breeders and asked them to walk about in the ring, flatten the grass. Who knows, in a hundred years this may be done as a ritual meeting of breeders, a sign of good will before the competitive judging begins. As they left to collect the sheep for the first class, I shouted after them,

'And don't think you will get away with bad-legged sheep, I can see their faults now!'

As with most judging, the pre-show mental preparations are soon made irrelevant. It is easy to tell yourself that the best sheep will win, to form a mental picture of the perfect animal. It is even possible to tell yourself which faults are most important to you, but real life is rarely so simple. Every sheep is unique, with its own blend of strengths and faults, which are never clear cut. Judging can easily become a compromise, in which you may dislike large parts of a sheep you have to put first, and, conversely, quite like another, whose isolated fault is so serious it must be placed down the order.

Some judges work on the 'minimum faults' formula. They look for the sheep with the least wrong with it and initially this may seem to be the obvious thing to do. The problem arises when this most fault-free animal is also lacking in strengths, in the points which are vital to the future of the breed. For example, a Texel ram should be well fleshed, especially in the hind quarters, where much high-priced meat is found. A ram with a well-filled hind leg will put more strain on his paston joint, which may then become weak. Should a judge mark it down for its weak paston joint or up for its well-filled hind leg? I have seen judges do both and both be equally convinced that they were right. I like to think that I am positive and look to mark up strengths rather than mark down faults, but then, it is always easy in the comfort of theory with no sheep to confound you.

A week after the Wilton Show, the whole family travelled down to the West Country. Vicki had been mentioning that we should have a summer holiday.

'We will', I said. 'We can travel down to Devon on Sunday and spend the day on the beach; on Monday I will judge the show; on Tuesday we can see the sale and travel North. Wednesday, we will travel from our overnight stop to see the Lanark show and the ram sale on Friday, before coming home.'

She did not agree that this constituted a summer holiday and, of course, she was right. But then we had one of the hottest days of the summer for the beach on Sunday and were down there in time for breakfast. Chris took the children for a second day of relaxation, while I prepared myself to judge the large entry of Texels. An added problem of judging in the South West is the great popularity of Dutch-type Texels in the region. I found myself with classes that included entries of the Dutch and French types, and many in between.

As the afternoon dragged into early evening, the final task of deciding which of the first-prize winners should become champion arrived. Should it be the big yearling ram with strong white masculine head and four good, sound legs supporting its well-fleshed body; or the smaller female, undoubtedly with some Dutch blood and with outstanding conformation and wool quality behind a very feminine and attractive head. The female took my eye, but she was not as well grown as she might have been, and perhaps her innate prettiness was blinding me from her lack of power. No, it must be the ram and I duly tapped him with my stick. After a show, I like to talk with exhibitors, explaining my actions when asked or just discussing points. I fell into conversation with the owner of the champion, who had a small flock in Somerset.

'Of course, he is sired by one of your rams', he mentioned, with a smile.

I felt totally embarrassed; it would not look well, though I had no regrets - he was the best sheep.

The next day, the champion and another from the same owner made top prices. I felt vindicated, the buyer is the real judge! The sire, a ram bought from me several years before as a lamb, had certainly done a good job. He, too, was in the sale; small flocks need to change their stock rams often and, with regret, the owner had sent him along. I had no hesitation in buying him. Such a chance to bring such a proven sire back within my own flock is a rare opportunity. Rufus was welcomed home.

We stopped on our journey north at Bolton to enjoy the swimming pool and sauna, a few moments of family break before the imposition of sheep and sheep breeders reasserted itself. We have made so many friends at Lanark that our annual visit is like going home. Whether we hope to buy or not, just to be there and see how the expensive rams of last year have bred and how their progeny sell is an event in itself. The facilities are old and, by modem standards, poor, yet the atmosphere that builds during the day is one with which no other auction can compete. I find myself coming home refreshed and rejuvenated. The main ram sale season awaits and I feel ready for it.

CHAPTER SEVEN

After the hectic months of July and August, September, although busy, settled into more of a pattern. The school holidays were all but over and a different breed of guest had taken to the road.

September is the busiest month on the farm. Our ram sales start in earnest and, with them, the hours of preparations and travel to many parts of the country. Breeding pedigree livestock is the most satisfying yet financially precarious of animal systems.

The satisfaction starts in the previous autumn, when the mating plans are worked out. Just as you and I, each ewe has its weak points as well as its strengths, and the selection of the right ram to correct those weaknesses, while maintaining and improving the strengths, is vitally important. Each year, you can picture that the combination of genes you have decided upon will produce the best lot of lambs the breed has ever known. The Meat and Livestock Commission, with their computerised figures and advanced technology, have told you that improvement is statistically certain.

Throughout the almost five-month period of sheep pregnancy, you strive to maintain maximum condition in your ewes. Paring their feet to prevent lameness, separating away the old, thin sheep to give them extra rations. Clearing the remaining grass from old summer pastures and then onto especially-grown crops of turnips to see them through the winter.

During the long, hard winter, the problems that come with every day are countered by the growing promise of the lamb crop to come. This is the time when dreams really develop. When new stock rams produce lambs with all their virtues and more besides, when the old retainers sire lambs, the likes of which they have never done before. Perhaps such dreams are unrealistic and, certainly, science is playing an even greater part in animal breeding; yet, even now, science can only work by statistical likelihood, by making better sheep more likely. Genetic variation maintains its almost limitless variability and, with it, the unexpected as well as the unlikely will always appear. Like winning the football pools, almost any ewe may breed in a winner.

She was a thin, old ewe but, as she reached the end of the sorting race, she looked at me with a determined glint in her eyes. I leant over and took her head, gently turning it so I could read her identification number.

'Ten years old, I bet you're getting a little short of teeth', I thought, and opened her mouth for a dental inspection. To my surprise they were all still there. I stood back and eyed her up and down. It was decision time for selecting the ewes fit enough for another season, a time when affection built up over many seasons' loyal service must be tempered with reality.

It would be unfair to the old ewe, as well as unwise on my pocket, to keep her too long. I was erring towards culling her out when my gaze settled on those determined eyes. I heard myself speak,

'Let her through, she can stay one more year'. Not wanting to move her further than necessary, I kept her with the small bunch in the paddock with the old stock ram. With increasing arthritis, he was a shadow of his former self, but, descended from one of the best early blood lines, he carried himself with regal dignity, a cut above the rest. The flock were scanned in November and, to my horror, the old ewe was carrying triplets.

'You silly old girl', I whispered loudly in her wrinkled ear. 'One would have been plenty for the likes of you.' She turned her head and looked at me again, a wise and knowing look.

She duly gave birth to triplets, two a little small but all fit and well. Two we left for her to rear, but one, a ram lamb, we reared on the bottle. Their growth was not tremendous but, as they grew, they showed the aristocratic qualities of their parents. They stood out from the crowd and, above all, they had those eyes. As sale time approached, the rams were sorted and, now over a year old, the two sons came forward for inspection. I considered sending them both to the same sale, but my need for a new stock ram and the uncertainty of finding one that I liked won the day. The smaller one, reared on the bottle, went to Wales, and sold for nearly a thousand guineas to a new breeder in the West Country.

As autumn comes round yet again, the success or otherwise of our ram and ewe selections the previous year become evident. Changes may be made in the light of this, new rams brought in and young ewes put to the ram for the first time. The computer printouts showing breeding traits going back several generations, as well as the ultra-sound scanner results showing the relative amounts of lean meat to fat and, of course, the growth rates, must all be checked through. And yet, at the end of the day, the final choice of which ram to put with which ewe must be my own. A gut feeling that does not knowingly consider any scientific data, but with it all carefully filed in the back of the mind, will say: 'that ram will go with that ewe'. I like to think that, even in this, romance is not dead.

~~~~~~~~~~~~~~~~~~~~

With the chill autumn nights getting ever-longer and the watery sun losing its strength, a new and hardy visitor comes to the door. This is the time of the spontaneous traveller. The one who looks up from his office desk on another drab Friday afternoon and decides he must get away. It is a time of young-minded people looking for fun. The telephone rang one lunch time.

'How many can you accommodate?', asked the young man as he poured over the symbols describing us in the farmhouse Bed and Breakfast guide.

This I found a very leading question and the latent wickedness in my mind pictured mountains of bodies filling every room. I regained my composure and replied.

'We have two double rooms and a family room; what combinations are you?'

After some thought and hurried background whispering, they booked all our rooms and rang off. A few minutes later, they phoned again.

'We are now ten, can you fit us in?' My mind pictured games of sardines and Whitehall farces.

'You know how many beds we have; it depends how well you know each other.'

'That will be fine, we will see you at eight', and the phone went dead.

They arrived after nine, but their infectious enthusiasm and joy of life soon wiped away any annoyance that they were late. They had booked a day at one of the new paintball war games sites that had become all the rage that year. As they went to their beds and I went to mine, I felt a mixture of envy at their liveliness and freedom, and joy at my own security, the meaning of which they would never understand. As I lay in my bed, I satisfied myself that I had escaped the complexities that their night must hold. On the other hand, the girls were very good-looking and perhaps it was just plain old-fashioned jealously that I really felt. They had booked breakfast for eight, and three of the lads and one girl duly arrived at the appointed hour.

'Mary is vegetarian and Jo doesn't eat sausage', said Peter, as Chris entered the room and after we had exchanged the good morning pleasantries.

'The rest will soon be down, I should just start cooking if I were you', Peter continued, in that friendly but positive tone that showed he was used to authority.

As they limped in, metaphorically, as well as physically in one case, I thought of old huntsmen returning home after a long, hard day in the saddle. They generally spoke few words but their eyes, although dulled and with that look of early disturbance, spoke volumes. Some were mentally prepared for the day. They sat, eating with relish and discussing war game tactics with Peter, but most were unsure whether they could spare the energy to lift the next forkful to their lips. The day that stretched ahead of the here and now was totally beyond them. These are not morning people, I thought. Would the war games kill them?

I need not have worried. Their life of fighting half of humanity on the daily grind into London and back had prepared them for far more than war games. They returned in the evening with differing tales but glowing with pride, as well as the remains of the paint. They were all single, and obviously so, bubbling with infectious joy and triviality.

'May we bring some drink in and have a little party? We want you to join us of, course', said a short and slightly balding young man, called John. John was obviously responsible for organising the evening events and seemed to have it well in hand.

We willingly agreed and soon the large fire at the end of the big Sitting Room was roaring to combat the early autumn chill. Bottles of all descriptions emerged from the boot of an old mini and were soon liberally distributed. I have often wondered just how many people who work in London are involved in marketing and quite what they actually market. Going by a straw poll of our guests, which is probably more scientifically random than most high-priced opinion polls, it must be nearly half the population. To whom do they market? Perhaps they all run around marketing to one another in ever-decreasing circles. Fortunately, I was interrupted from taking this view to any conclusion by a bottle, held by Susie, a tall blonde with the most captivating deep blue eyes. 'You could sell me anything', I thought, as I allowed her to poor me another glass of red wine.

She sat down and asked me about the farm - did we keep cows or corn? Words rolled from her lips with eloquent smoothness, as I struggled to think of an interesting reply. Peter's group were discussing their next holiday. Their conversation would rise, settle, break out in raucous laughter and then gently build again, as though the humour had momentarily taken the wind from their conversation.

'When are you due back at the hospital, Susie, Monday morning?', asked Peter, sitting up in his chair and looking in our direction.

Susie nodded and added a few succinct views on holidays. Chris had reappeared with one of the girls and John, carrying the few 'nibbles' she said she would provide, which looked more like a steaming feast.

'Are you training to be a nurse?', I asked Susie, anxious for the conversation not to die.

'No, I'm a doctor', she replied, as she took her bowl of chili and slice of dripping garlic bread. John stood above us, food tray in hand.

'Susie's more than a doctor, she's our resident brain surgeon', he said, as he turned away.

I looked for somewhere to hide and hoped I had found it in a large bite from my garlic bread. To my cost, I discovered a seemingly complete clove of garlic and hastily took a deep gulp of my wine.

'This is a lovely house', said Susie, changing the subject, obviously embarrassed at my embarrassment.

They were still partying at two when I left for my bed. Chris was still going strong, but she has always been a night owl. 'Well,' I thought as I snuggled between the sheets, 'if ever my brain grows as big as my feet, I know where to go for treatment', and I switched off the light.

A high percentage of our guests are from the colonies, returning to the civilisation of the old country for a refresher course in courtesy and traditional standards. Among these are a fair smattering of farmers, who are always more than anxious to swap moans. It is important to be able to compete in the 'life is harder for me' stakes and, for this, some preparation is necessary. Never allow farms to be described in square miles and make sure American guests know that our corn includes all grains, not just maize.

One June afternoon, we had just finished shearing and the last batch of ewes had turned the wrong way upon release from the shed. They were heading for the house and the open plan gardens beyond when they were intercepted by some intrepid New Zealanders and turned into the field. The two couples were from the South Island and, needless to say, sheep farmers. My father, who had been helping with the sheep, joined us for his fortified cup of tea and a chat with the guests. He had visited New Zealand on a two-week tour during a trip to Australia several years before and was now an authority. Chris showed the wives to their rooms whilst I made a fresh pot of tea. On their return, the men were missing.

'Oh, Dad has taken them to see the flock', I said. The ladies looked at their watches and laughed.

'Less than three hours in the country and we have already lost them to a bunch of sheep.'

Wherever in the world a farmer lives, he is suffering the same basic problems. A market, which the last war made secure and supported, had declined whilst efficiency had increased. The result is reduced prices and thus a need to further increase yields to maintain total income. At the same time, public awareness of the environment has put pressures and restrictions on production, which are claimed as sensible. 'After all, we have too much corn anyway', the message continues. The only problem is that reduced yields and more restrictions don't pay the bills. One day, the fact that beauty doesn't just happen but must be paid for will sink home. I hope it happens while there is still some beauty and some farmers left, and not just huge estates run by economic-minded managers with no social conscience.

8

CHAPTER EIGHT

The valley which forms the southern boundary of the farm also gives us the slopes and meadows that are needed in a good sporting farm. All wildlife is maintained and kept in balance. As part of this, we encourage and shoot pheasant and partridge, and welcome the hunt to draw for foxes. The crows and magpies that destroy thousands of nests annually are kept in check and the result is an area bubbling with life and sound.

The countryside as we know it is a man-made environment and has been for hundreds of years. Tradition may be out of fashion today, but, without it, much of that which we love the countryside for would be lost. Many would like us to simply take the 'best' bits and keep them in isolation, like pickles in a jar. Fortunately, most who live in or understand the countryside know it is, and must be, dynamic. That controlling foxes is as important as planting oak woods, that the shooting of pheasants encourages more small birds and that the ongoing equation is dependent on ongoing management by man. I hope most of those who enjoy our paradise know that it is not a fantasy, but a reality where hard decisions have to be made. This does not make the beauty any less beautiful, or the harmony less harmonious, but it does make the total responsibility of us all even more important.

Parts of the world do not share our tradition for sporting fair play. The environment may exist for the sole use of man and little else. Beauty and balance may be words with a different meaning in the national context, and responsibility used as a means of showing domination rather than care. One American guest with a small farm on the wooded lower slopes of the Rocky Mountains comes instantly to mind. The breakfast conversation had come round to shooting - or hunting, as the Americans put it. I was trying to explain that the challenge of achieving a difficult and sporting kill was far more important than the number of kills achieved. I was obviously speaking to deaf ears.

'Turkey, do you shoot turkey?', the man interrupted, in a loud voice.

'No, not turkey', I replied. 'Pheasant and partridge, mostly.'

'How about quail?', the man ventured. 'Do you shoot quail?'

'They occasionally breed here, but we don't shoot them.'

'We shoot quail. They're quick, damned quick. You gotta shoot 'em from the hip.'

Feeling this wasn't either safe or particularly sporting, I tried to explain to him the British rural environment, where the thrill of challenging and, if necessary, killing a wild animal in its home ground is a traditional part of real conservation and balance.

We try to weight the dice in favour of the game, placing cover crops on high ground, placing guns in low and poorly sited spots, and hoping for good, windy conditions. When all are met, we move off for the first drive, guns standing at their numbered marker pegs, waiting, checking guns and cartridges, stamping on the frozen ground to keep warm and loosen stiff muscles. Sparrows buzz in a flock, bouncing down the hedge line and sounding the alarm. Pigeons take wing from a top field and circle the valley.

A guest at the other end of the line fires a ranging shot. The pigeons rise higher, but none fall. The shot brings the dreaming to an end. Two guests nearby, who have been sharing a joke, hastily take their places, then silence returns. The beaters can be heard now, the constant tapping of their sticks, the whistling of the dog handlers rising above the steady tap-tap of the stop, long in position in the hedge above us.

At last, a big cock pheasant rises laboriously into the air. He appears to be heading for the third guest in the line, as he leans back and lets the air swirling in the valley lift him. He then seems to lean back even more, rising almost vertically and letting the cross current carry him across the line. Suddenly, the fifth gun realises he is passing over him and not his friend standing on the other side of the hedge. He quickly flings his gun up and into an arc, following the bird's flight, but as he tries to swing through the bird, it catches a stronger current and lets itself go, now flying in a sharp, curving climb that is too quick for the human below. Both barrels are fired, but the shot passes harmlessly behind the bird. The guests on either side see their fellow is beaten and fire a final salvo in a desperate attempt to bag this fine old bird. But, as the pheasant settles into a glide and disappears gently behind the wood on the far hill, they know that they were too slow. The day continues, some birds coming down, but most climbing on to the safety of a distant wood or cover.

Over a bowl of soup at lunch time or in the evening, as we wait for the smell of roast beef to materialise into the real thing, tales of the ones that got away are shared and elaborated. Good shots are quizzed as to how they missed so often, and new guests are praised for any successes. Quickly, the event takes on the atmosphere of cosy laughter around the fire. Too soon the evening will be over. The table a thing of empty plates and empty bottles, the chairs filled with old men and old aches fighting their inclination to settle and sleep. In the morning, as I travel around the farm, sparrows will be back in their hedges and the pigeon on the wing. Some pheasants will already have returned and, within a couple of days, most will be back in their favourite patch.

As the year moves round and February arrives, the shooting season comes to an end. Pheasants appear in numbers hitherto unknown. A cock pheasant struts boldly by me in full mating plumage and herds his harem of hen birds up the nearby hedge. He stops to peck at an appetizing worm and then looks at me, opens his wings and airs them with several threatening flaps. As he turns away again, unhurried and in total command, I am reminded very firmly that he won the winter's contest and will not let me forget it. Migrating birds use the cover crops to rest and feed, making it a haven of life at a hungry time.

My mind drifted back to the previous Easter and the weekly gatherings of the Bible group during Lent. I had offered the farmhouse as a meeting place and ten or so individuals were drawn around the fire. In an attempt to link our daily routine with the idea of prayer, we were individually outlining our day and the important parts of it. The primary school teachers were united in their intensity and conviction; for some it had gone well, for others pandemonium. The retired felt embarrassed that their day revolved around relative trivia, but were soon persuaded that nothing is trivia to the almighty. As my turn arrived, they seemed prepared for a major statement. I didn't want to disappoint them.

'My day started at four thirty', I began, drawing accompanying nods of the appreciation and respect. I looked around, banged the table and, breaking into a broad grin, exclaimed, 'Because that's the time the world cup cricket match started on the radio.'

The party looked bemused, they had wanted me to start work then, had prepared themselves for it. Many guests inquire about my working day, finding the meeting of a real farmer unsettling for their preconceived ideas. The fact that I endeavour not to have two days the same complicates the issue.

As a one-man show, I don't have to plan my day around other staff.

My mealtimes can be arranged around my stomach as much as my wife and thus I gain extra flexibility. I have an innate fear of becoming the servant of my work and of routine. I am determined to maintain that work is achieved in the order that I decide daily, not because that is the way it has always been done. Work must always be the servant of man and not the other way around.

As with most people, I get up as late as I can. On a cold winter's morning, with sleet rolling across my window, I may not move from my bed till the increasing light dents my conscience. In summer, a walk around the farm as the sun throws patterns across the cobweb-dewed grass sets me up for the day.

Within this happy mastery of my environment there are, of course, times when life is not so simple and idyllic. During lambing in late February, a midnight check on the yard of heavily pregnant ewes may locate a sheep who looks uneasy, standing and sitting, walking in circles, scratching the ground and calling for a non-existent lamb. Classical signs of imminent birth. I go indoors and make a coffee, bide an hour, and check again. She looks more imminent, more uneasy but it is not ready yet. I go to bed and set my alarm, its droll tones dragging me from my heavenly bliss. I search the yard, where is she? I rub my eyes clearing the sleep, tripping over obvious obstructions and cursing, as I try to take in the light and situation. I finally find her, blissfully resting under a hay rack. Happily chewing, she will look up, as if to say: 'Lamb, me, tonight? Oh no, I decided to wait until tomorrow.'

Amidst the mastery and dominance that I assert over my estate, it's not only my livestock that like to have a say. There is an unfortunate factor called conscience that constantly tries to rear its head. Take a similar night during the lambing season. I have retired to bed, confident that no ewes will give birth before dawn. I have gone to sleep and the world is at peace. I will suddenly wake in the early hours with an irrational desire to check a lamb born the previous day. I tell myself that I checked it during the evening, and all was well, so I should just go to sleep. I almost settle, but then the dulling embers burst into flames: 'But you didn't check it at midnight!' There is no alternative but to get up and look at this poor animal, which is, needless to say, sleeping.

'What are you doing today?' has become a comment I dread hearing at breakfast. Innocent enough on the surface, I know it to contain mountainous pitfalls, whatever answer I give. If I reply positively, dredging my mind for every job that needs doing, I will turn a sunny morning into one so overcast with unpleasant tasks that I regret not succumbing to flu during the night. If, on the other hand, I cheerfully allow myself to be on top of my work, I know a multitude of domestic chores or revisions to the forty-year house-improving plan will be passed my way. The only way is to remain slightly above these ups and downs, as a captain on the bridge of his ship in a strong sea and wait for the squall to pass.

If I am totally honest, I will admit that any decisions not made for me by my livestock or my conscience, will be made by the weather or politicians, yet, if I let this train of thought take over, I know that I will soon feel pressurised in so many directions that I won't know if I am coming or going. No, I convince myself that, despite all these factors, I really am the boss. When I walk round the stock before breakfast or feed them in the yard early on a winter's morning; when I mow a field of hay or take stock to market; when I mend a fence or decide to take an hour off, it is because I have decided to do so and no one else.

My great-grandfather bought the farm in the 1920's, though various ancestors had been farmers here for a hundred years before that. The collection of papers, carefully stored over the years, gives a vivid description of the farm as it was and how it has evolved. As generations have come, imposed their personalities and gone, the basic farm, with its timeless buildings and light, grateful land, has been unchanged. Certainly, small variations, additions and subtractions are part of the determinations of every generation to leave something uniquely theirs for posterity. But, beneath it all, is the knowledge that we are but ants on a lump of granite and, in the context of time, no more important.

'Live as if you will die tomorrow and farm as if you will live forever' is a saying often voiced. The imposition of 'custodian' is something that farmers are very aware of in their private and personal way, but which few non-farmers can hope to comprehend. The wind of change that has blown through urban life in recent years, replacing gentlemen's agreements with gazumping, and demanding that economics become the sole God in this supposedly Christian land, is now threatening to blow away the fabric of rural life too. The fact that rural roots are deeper makes the fear of failure so much more profound.

I often wonder if the peasants thrown out in the time of the great enclosures or the Scotsmen disturbed in the Highland clearings felt as we do. Those who are young enough and lucky enough will be able to adapt; those who have no conscience will sell their souls and become urban managers who happen to have farms. The rest will be as martyrs at the stake and I fear their passing will be no less painful. The tightrope of being able to adapt and succeed in this modern, harsh environment and yet remain loyal to one's duty as a custodian is one I am finding it increasingly difficult to walk.

In many ways, this book is a log of my efforts. At the outset, our farm could have been the same as it was a hundred years ago. The breeds of stock have changed, the horses become tractors and I have become a working farmer, when my ancestors would have had scores of men for the purpose. But, beneath it all, the farm has the same attitude and relies on the same balance of agricultural crops for its survival. I look upon it as my duty to try to encompass the demands of modern man with the traditional values that have held the farm together for so long. Without these values, we would have no farm; with them, perhaps I will find the imagination to succeed.

9

CHAPTER NINE

As the year rolled on and Christmas approached, the flow of guests became a trickle. The old farmhouse was not fully centrally heated; though the fire in the Breakfast Room had a radiator system to air the bedrooms, the corridors remained on the cool side. The roof had been re-laid at the turn of the century and now several holes had appeared. It carried no insulation and at night I could count the stars between the slates. Though little but driven rain or snow would come in, most of any heat would soon go out.

This is a good time of year for taking stock, pulling your ideas and dreams together and looking for the path ahead. We had been doing Bed and Breakfast for a year and had liked it. The work had been hard for Chris, but the thanks of satisfied guests and the improvement in our children, now both at private school, had been such that we wanted to continue.

'We had over eighty in August!', sparked Chris, looking up from her reservation diary with the glow of success. Indeed, there was much for her to feel good about.

'The number of guests will fall now, especially if it's wet and cold, but the children will be back soon, and then it will be Christmas.' A look of tired fulfilment spread across her face.

'The rams are sold, the ewes are out with the stock rams, all is at peace with the world.' I allowed myself a mock grin and let my chin rest in my hands, and my elbows on the old table. I could easily have let myself go, wallowed in dreams that come so easily, especially here.

'Well, we can't all sit around all day', I said, mischievously, and set off to solve some of the problems I knew waited for me outside.

'Off to move the ewe hoggs before lunch, back about one.' Chris, still analysing her book, gave an almost imperceptible nod. As I walked the sheep, I set to thinking too; there was much to analyse.

Improvements were certainly needed. The kitchen and the sitting rooms wanted an overhaul, the children their own rooms, some rooms required en-suite facilities and greater flexibility and, most of all, we needed a new roof. I had always been told that the most important part of any house was the roof, so we started there.

If we put on a new one, we could refurbish the attic space as extra bedrooms for the children. Then we could put en-suite facilities in the existing rooms - they were certainly big enough - slap on a bit of paint and Bob's your uncle. This idea had some merit and it was progressive. I told myself that it would give us much more potential, save on heating bills, be fairer to the children and increase the value of the house.

The main problem came when I tried to do the costings. They didn't add up or, rather, they added up to far too much. Upon my return, I sat down to list my thoughts. I turned over a new page in the old diary that was serving as a minute book. Let us bring the farm into the reckoning. Over recent years, we have built up the size of the flock and have some good young females coming on. We never do well selling females at the main sales, as our sheep from our light, stony soil are never as big or strong as those from rich dairy parts of the country. But, if we selected some good young ewes and added some of the ewe lambs that will be born next spring, we would have enough for a sale here on the farm.

The buyers would only be able to compare like with like, and they could appreciate the land they had been reared on. My grandfather bred dairy cows and had his best sales here, on the farm. I shared my thoughts with Chris.

'When would you have it?', she asked, with growing interest.

'Oh, I don't know, but it must be sufficiently late on for the ewe lambs to be big enough.'

If we left it until October, we could have put the ewes to the ram already. That might appeal to the new breeders, who want new blood lines without buying a ram and by October they should have some harvest money in.

'Yes, I think October of next year feels right. It would give us time to prepare the sheep during the summer and plan to have a new roof before Christmas. That way, we wouldn't disturb the house while we were busy with guests.'

This sort of progressive idea can easily go the way of many nocturnal ideas. The infectious enthusiasm that comes with its seeming ability to cure all problems can dissolve, as its disadvantages, overlooked during the excitement, come to light. In this case, they didn't, so I went looking for them. But the more I thought of the on-farm sale idea, the more I liked it. It would be a gamble and the costs would be high, but the potential was there, and I felt confident. It gave us something to work towards.

The leaking roof and cold corridors seemed less bad when we could see improvements ahead. We were planning the sale in good time, which was important, and we could manage some work on the kitchen and a lick of paint to go on with. I would consult the auctioneers. All these ideas must have been in my mind as separate parcels, isolated by their individual problems and that separation unrecognised as a potential strength. As the evening drew on and tiredness came, I felt a few pangs of doubt, but only a few. By the morning, they had gone, and the weak winter sun had more purpose in it. Tomorrow seemed a brighter day.

~~~~~~~~~~~~~~~~~

Harry often called in for a drink and a dose of 'social intercourse', as he called it. The biggest extrovert I have ever met, he runs his own photography business and, as we were en route between his studio and home, we were well-placed for a pit stop. He had been a guest here on several shoots and knew of Chris's culinary skills. As Secretary of the local vintage car drivers' club, he had the job of organising the Christmas lunch and I soon put two and two together. Despite his flamboyance, he has a natural fear of offending and broached the subject with the confidence of Oliver, asking for more.

'We won't arrive until one, as we're stopping in Banbury for coffee and then making our way here by the back roads. How many? Oh, about fifty.' Chris was several stops ahead of him and had already calculated that to be the maximum number the Sitting Room could take, when stripped of easy chairs and set as two long tables.

They arrived in convoy, two Sundays before Christmas, seventeen old Austins, gleaming and carefully parked in front of the old house.

We had spent much of the previous afternoon clearing away the regular furniture and setting up the temporary tables and chairs. A Christmas tree was put up in the corner between the fireplace and the window. We had used the long room for dining on few, but nevertheless, very memorable occasions. Always for a large gathering and invariably, my memory tells, with large characters. For just twenty or so, a single table down the centre of the room would suffice, with enough room for the group of chairs around the fire to be left in place. A larger number required two rows of tables and relied on the buzz of its fullness, rather than balance, for its atmosphere. The former allowed more room and became more expansive in every way, the latter was cosy. Both worked well, but it was vital not to fall between the two.

I collected the folding tables and stacking chairs from the sports hall at the far end of the village, enjoying the gentle purr of the old tractor, as I negotiated the tightly-parked cars and contemplated the work of setting up the tables. Any person harbouring the notion that arranging tables and chairs for fifty is a straightforward operation should attend our next function. Logically, a little pre-planning should save a lot of work.

Chris stood in the doorway. 'How long are they? Try three up that side.' I manoeuvred the tables into position, arranged the chairs as I saw fit. Fit was the wrong word.

'Oh no, that table leg is in the way, no one could sit there.' The line of tables and chairs was moved to and fro'. Here, 'too close to the fire'; there, 'not enough room for the servers to get around'. Finally, the two rows were assembled. Incongruous in their grey plastic and tubular metal, but assembled. I could see Chris was not happy and developed a sudden desire to check the sheep grazing on Worcester Hill.

'Do you think they would look better facing the other way?' Chris looked at me intensely. I searched my conflicting mind for a rational statement.

'Well?', she said, a few impatient seconds later, taking my delay as indifference.

It felt wrong, I couldn't see it working, but I knew just to say so without clear-cut reasons would be taken as negative thinking and idleness. I could picture Chris receiving my 'No' with an 'All right, I'll do it myself'. Yet, to meekly go through the motions of moving every table and chair, just for the mental satisfaction of being told, 'No, it was better before' and the knowledge that it would all have to be put back again seemed wrong, un-masculine, illogical.

'Let's try that corner and see how it feels', I compromised.

'I don't think it will all fit that way', was the response. Nevertheless, we tried, agreed it was wrong and finally achieved an assembly that we had never tried before and could certainly never produce again.

By the evening, Chris was hard at work unfolding tablecloths and laying tables. First, the cutlery, separated by side plates, then the napkins and table decorations and, finally, the crackers, without which no Christmas lunch could be complete. The tree, which reached to the ceiling, glowed in the firelight, its red and silver tinsel cascading light onto the mirror opposite. As the evening came to an end and we headed for bed, we took a final look. It seemed so settled in the gentle light of the dying fire, as if it had always been so. The incongruity of the table was now lost under the old heavy linen tablecloths, the plastic of the chairs mellowed by the symmetry and the fluctuating glow of the fire. From such empty chaos had come such peace. We put our arms around each other in the doorway and supported each other's tiredness. I spoke my thoughts. 'It looks so peaceful now, it won't see much of that tomorrow.' Too tired to reply, Chris walked knowingly to bed.

The morning came so soon, with the sheep to be fed and the two big turkeys already scenting the kitchen air. Eleanor and her sister Ruth were to be waitresses and, with James and Vicki to serve the drinks and my parents on hand to help, we were well prepared. A side table had been set in the corner of the big Sitting Room by the door and, when all were seated, the two turkeys were carried, steaming and trophy-like, into the room.

So often today, turkey is machine sliced, almost transparent and preheated to go further and make life easier. A meal can be almost finished before enough meat has been eaten for the taste buds to realise it has started. We had decided this was not for us. We would begin with the right anticipation.

'One turkey will not be enough', Chris had proclaimed, the ensuing problem being how and where to cook the second bird. 'A friend in need is a friend indeed', thought Chris, and approached Alison, whose small, stone house stood just fifty yards up the road. Alison was away, which meant her hard-working doctor husband, Simon, rousing himself from his bed in the early hours, lest the timer on the oven failed. 'How great is friendship,' I mused.

The table seemed to groan under the weight of the birds. I looked up and along at the lines of faces, glowing with anticipation. Children bouncing, fathers with funny hats already askew, mothers fussing. They had enjoyed their meal before the first forkful lifted from a plate. There was no time for self-praise, but I enjoyed the carving. The meal came and was gone, and Harry rose to his feet. Amid clearing plates and the crackling fire he gave out his silly prizes for best costume and slowest car, and then came the raffle with prizes galore. Finally, he turned to Chris and smiled wickedly. James had crept outside and now stood at the door. He moved forward cradling a large, domestic goose.

'For you', said Harry, breaking with the party into noisy rapture. 'His mate is outside. We couldn't kill them, so you can put them on your lake.'

As the gathering dissolved into the garden and the vintage cars left for their return journey, we took the old Land Rover and released the geese on the lake. When we returned, the tables had been cleared and lunch laid for the helpers in the breakfast room. As we ate our lunch, the clock struck four, the rush of the day crept over us and we felt exhausted. The food took away the sharpness and left us feeling numb but satisfied. We had served fifty with no complaints, a few comments, and a wealth of genuine thanks.

'See you next year!', they had said - and meant it.

We only had two guests in the run-up to Christmas; a quiet, young couple, who were on their way to visit relatives down south. They soon retired to their room and left us to ourselves. The children had revelled in their first few days of holiday but were now showing the classic signs of being overtired. James would not go to bed. I had reached the stage where my gentle admiration for his delaying tactics would have to be superseded by wifely support. James and his mother have always shared similar humour, but I could see that on this occasion Chris's was wearing a bit thin.

'Go to bed', I said, firmly, rising from the sofa. James reached the door and turned, another tactic having come to mind. I nipped it in the bud,

'GO TO BED!' James left and closed the door, only to return quickly. This time he ignored my command and said,

'But there is water pouring into your office.'

The little sitting room adjacent doubled as my office, with an old, roll-top desk in the corner. At first I thought that, if nothing else, his school had taught him the art of delay to a very high standard, but then realised he was right. Water was cascading through the blistering ceiling paper and over my files, some of it finding its way noisily into the tin litter bin alongside. The bathroom is immediately above, and I turned to Chris with growing anger, picturing a guest with excessive water in the bath.

'Tell him to let some water out, quickly.'

She rushed up the stairs only to come down much more slowly.

'Well?', I said.

'They're both in the bath', she muttered, shocked to virtual silence.

'But did you tell them to let some water out?', I continued, in an effort to keep proceedings concentrating on the salvation of my office. As I spoke, they had clearly realised the situation and water could be heard rushing into the drain outside. The water entering the office slowly subsided and then stopped.

A strange silence settled, broken only by hushed shuffling from the room above and the soundless noise of water percolating. James had gone to bed; he knew when to disappear.

'I'll get some old towels to soak up the water', shouted Chris, disappearing towards the kitchen. I looked up at the ceiling.

'Will you stay, or will you come down?', I said aloud. As if in answer a final drop of water struck the side of the metal bin, echoing loudly.

A few years earlier, we had suffered a similar problem with a shower. The ceiling seemed settled; the paper had ballooned with water, but the plaster had not moved. Not until the morning after a New Year's party, with half our crockery and all our glass neatly stacked beneath. As if designed to fully heighten an insurer's doubts, it had then descended with total accuracy.

'I don't trust you.' My memory inspired my decision and I cleared the landing strip for the plaster. 'Just in case', I muttered, as I switched off the light.

We discovered it was not the bathers' fault; that the plumber, who had been re-laying some tiles earlier that day, had forgotten to reconnect the overflow, so that every time a rhythmic wave had hit the overflow, it had been re-routed on to my office desk. No permanent harm was done and even the decidedly sheepish look on our guests' faces when they came down to breakfast mellowed as they enjoyed their bacon and egg.

~~~~~~~~~~~~~~~~~~~~

Our family has many branches. Of these, many individuals have become well-known over the years, particularly as farmers and often as bad farmers. Fortunately, some moved outside the county or took up other professions, and it is undoubtedly from among these that the more interesting characters emerge, save one or two exceptions, who stand out like sore thumbs on an aging body. The best qualities of the family have generally been passed through the female line.

Cousin Cynthia, with her Austrian-born doctor husband and four delicious daughters, returned to the county when I was very young. I was, however, not too young to notice these lovely creatures, whom time has shown to have great intelligence and personality, as well as beauty.

I courted Diana, the eldest, for a time during my college years, and shared the company of the next two girls, Celia and Hillary, whenever the opportunity arose. Chris had become a friend of Hillary through Young Farmers Club activities long before we met, which cemented our family bonds. Hillary was a romantic, who threw herself at whatever she was doing with complete abandon. She became a well-qualified nurse, chef and actress before her twentieth birthday, and we knew that it was only a matter of time before she threw herself at a man in the same fashion. Whether mankind was ready for this, I doubted, but was highly envious of this fellow, whoever he was, still innocently going about his business.

It happened during a holiday to Australia and the victim was a six-foot-five trainee Australian doctor. With the spell cast, she returned home, he followed shortly and proposed after two days. Her father had been ill and told to rest and we were wondering what we could do to help. Hillary had phoned earlier in the day and asked to call, in that lovely, bubbly way of hers, which makes a visit sound like a royal request.

They came for lunch, Quintin unfolding from the car like some automatically extending ladder. The events of the holiday in Australia, the travel and their return, flowed as on warm air carried by the total passion that gripped them and all they touched. The wedding would be next August, I heard her say, as I returned from a distant daydream.

Where were we now, oh yes, December, I should have known, as the sound of a sleet shower rolled across the window. Quintin must be feeling it, I thought, so fresh from his Australian summer. The discussion had carried on during my mental digression and Chris was asking how we could help. Hillary smiled a knowing smile. She knew exactly how she would like us to help. She hadn't changed. I smiled back and hoped she never would.

'Could you possibly put up the bridegroom, his family, the best man and his girlfriend for a week before the wedding?' She took our silence as acceptance and continued.

'And, oh yes, can we have the party after the wedding at your place?' Such a request from almost anyone else would have been met with a look of total incredulity. But we took it as a great honour, one only a real friend could ask of another, and looked forward to a wonderful time.

'What are you doing tonight?', Chris asked, changing the subject abruptly now that the real business of the visit had been agreed. The lovers looked at each other and Chris continued. 'We are going to the Yuletide Ball, why not come too?'

It was instantly agreed, and a handful of minor obstacles came up for resolution. A phone call obtained extra tickets, Hillary located a ball gown in the depths of her memory and only the question of a dinner jacket for Quintin remained. At six-foot-five, with a forty-two-inch chest and thirty-two-inch waist it was not going to be easy. We instantly thought of big Jim, an ex-England lock-forward who farmed at the other end of the village, and his suit was duly borrowed. The jacket was fine, if slightly short in the sleeve, but the trousers were a different thing. Quintin stood in the kitchen with a big fold of trouser in front of him doing a Coco the Clown impersonation. He turned.

'Hillary, we could both get in here!' A pair of bright red braces were borrowed from Hillary's father and we were ready for what promised to be a mad evening.

Yuletide balls are historic and have traditionally been gatherings of large numbers of fun-loving young farmers just before Christmas. We had not been to one for a couple of years and soon noticed it was now a far more serious and well-behaved event than it had been in the days when we were part of the organising committee. Through a blur of revelry, lubricated by a small drink, we agreed a certain amount of enlivenment was needed.

We were part of a long table of about thirty people. I sat at the end of a long side and was wagered that I would not crawl under the table for its full length, remove a shoe from the girl at the end, and return. I was amazed, not that I was groped, but by whom?

As I emerged above table level, I realised that history had moved on in my absence and that world war three had now begun. Rolls, the eternal standby, were the first artillery to be used in retaliation to attacks from a neighbouring table. As ammunition ran short, ice from the G and Ts or driver's orange juice and, finally, hot mince pies joined the fray. My final memory of the short but sharp encounter was of a hot mince pie hitting Libby, the beautiful girl on my right, just above her cleavage, breaking up and rapidly trickling where hot mince pie is not meant to trickle. The dancing got underway and Quintin removed his jacket, the bright red braces taking the strain as he jived to the music.

'Raffle tickets, one pound a strip', a young man said, as he passed Chris.

Without speaking, Chris handed him a pound and started to undress him, passing pieces of clothing to different people as they danced by. She stopped at his underpants and socks and danced away. He came running over.

'What about my clothes?' She shrugged her shoulders and danced on.

Hillary and Quintin returned home in the morning. We knew Hillary of old; now we knew Quintin carried a similar wit and madness, a great joy of life. 'Roll on August', I thought, 'this is going to be one hell of a wedding'.

~~~~~~~~~~~~~~~~~

I love Christmas. Not just for the break for festivity in the bleak mid-winter or for any of the individual moments that grow warmly in the memory, but for the overall feeling of giving. A time when no one should have anything to prove, when the hostilities of modern life should take a back seat. Competition is a word that must hover very near the surface of everyday living, but it can spoil it, like a sharp breeze over the water of a calm sunny day. At Christmas, it should be pushed away, the metaphorical slippers replacing the metal-toe-capped wellingtons and people able to relax into their real selves. However, this need not bring the best out in everyone and family reunions can be hell.

Chris is one of a family of six and for many years we joined in the celebrations with her parents. They were a wonderful couple and I will remember the generosity and selflessness of Chris's mum for as long as I live. However, the divergence of attitude and opinion between the family and their partners with one another was not always peaceful. The day might start in the right spirit but become rather more spirited as it developed, and the journey home was often one of great relief.

Our first Christmas in the farmhouse was memorable. So much more space and more atmosphere. The large Sitting Room seemed made for Christmas, but where to put the tree? By the door in the corner next to the old inglenook fireplace with its copper to reflect the lights, or next to the other fire in the corner? No! That would be too hot. Finally, we decided by the outside wall, between the two central windows. Cool enough to hold its needles for as long as possible, visible from both the hall and outside, central to the room and glorious when seen reflected in the full-length mirror from my chair by the fire. Vicki was an ace at tree decorations, especially when spurred on by constructive criticism from her ever-helpful brother.

We are never organised for Christmas. I claim it is part of the relaxed approach necessary to fully appreciate the occasion, but it is probably more to do with my natural disorganisation. Shopping seems to start on Christmas Eve and decorations and present wrapping are rarely finished before we rush off to church at midnight. I can appreciate some might prefer to be ready, to feel everything is in its place before the day can begin. Fortunately, I have never wanted such, and revel in the chaos and glory of spontaneity.

Stockings are definitely a good invention, especially at Christmas, when they form an early morning diversion for the children. That is not to say that I have never been diverted by a stocking or its contents, but at Christmas, heralded by a very short night and little sleep, they are definitely welcome, if a bit lumpy.

The part of Christmas about which Chris is adamant is the opening of presents. This must always and only be done under the tree when everyone is there. At first, I thought this contrary to my 'let everything hang out' approach to the day but the joy, or sometimes otherwise, of seeing every person open their presents continually brings out the giving part of Christmas. When this has to wait for me to feed the stock, us all to attend Church and my parents to return from a visit to my brother and family, it can be well into the morning.

The best part of anything is the looking forward to it, but try telling that to a young child, who has been eying an interestingly shaped parcel from a far-off aunt. At this time, the word 'child' must mean anyone young enough to breathe and I would argue against anyone who suggests that maturity means being less childlike. As can be imagined, there is no lunch time. Lunch just happens when it is ready, and everyone is assembled. Many will be so filled by sampling their presents or so tired of smelling the food wafting increasingly from the kitchen, that their appetites will have deserted them.

Kay would join us after church. The widow of an old family friend, she had come to share in our lunch and our festivities. 'Christmas is for children', I have often heard said. Well, not only children. The look on an old lady's face as she sees children open their presents, as she remembers her youth, is sometimes far more poignant.

One thing Chris did inherit from her mother is her generosity, and this is especially so in the selection of vegetables at Christmas. As one who has never been excited by any vegetables, I have often regretted this waste of her open nature. There must have been other ways of showing she cared. Post-lunch, Christmas is a chair-bound occasion, unless visitors call with last-minute presents or children decide they need partners for a new game.

There is little to differentiate a farmhouse Christmas from any other kind at this time of day. A chair is a chair, and a man sleeping in it is much like any other. If he has done a morning's work in the early hours, he may feel he has deserved it and he may avoid the nagging conscience to get up and walk off his lunch. Nevertheless, the deep, satisfied snore will be the same and so will the derisory comments it receives. In the end, the farmer will have to rise to the call of the sheep or the bellow of the cows, unless he can find a willing volunteer.

'James.' A voice from the depths of sleep, trying to be considerate, but firm, will utter from my chair. 'Go and feed the sheep, there's a good lad.' The body in the chair opposite, which had moments before shown signs of life, has nearly stopped breathing. There is no response. I risk opening an eye briefly.

'James', says Chris in support, 'Your father wants you to feed the sheep.' Some moments later, a voice will come:

'In a minute, where is the food?'. He rises, laboriously, sarcastically looking for sympathy, pitying my increasing old age.

'The corn is on the trailer, the hay is in the barn.' I let him leave before I open my eyes and then smile, 'What a good lad, how about another cup of tea, mum?', but Chris is now settled in James's chair and too wise to move.

Farming can be condescendingly described as a way of life and usually as an entry to justify its poor return on capital, much as nurses should work for a pittance. It is certainly a way of life, in that throughout your farming life you can never get far away from it; weekends, bank holidays and especially Christmas all fall victim to it. However much preparation you do, the actual work of feeding sheep, milking cows and generally checking all is well must be done on the day.

I got up before dawn with the intention of an early start and a quick finish. I lit the fire as the tea brewed and, before I had finished my cup, it was out. Three attempts later, a smoky glow amid hissing wood did not auger well. As my feelings lost their seasonality, my nose picked up the scent that only comes from a housebound cat. I found the evidence behind the door and had just finished scrubbing the floor when the phone rang. Phones always have a different, more laboured, ring when they herald tidings of disaster. Indeed, the rams had escaped and were making their way up the road.

'Should they be?', the caller finished with remarkable sincerity.

My three disasters behind me, I felt well set for the day. As I walked through the steady drizzle, which was rapidly becoming heavy rain, en route to my breakfast and the onset of Christmas, I felt a strange benevolence for the darkened houses and drawn curtains. They had already missed half the day.

The village is a wonderful community for Christmas, everyone knows everyone and can wish them well with absolute sincerity, if not total honesty. The grey stone houses and winding streets sloping down to the river are the things of Christmas cards. Only once in my lifetime have they been snow-covered and, as I sat in my fireside chair trying not to watch the Wizard of Oz for the tenth time, I remembered it.

I must only have been sixteen or so and Christmas Eve found us in our normal chaotic state. The presents had been wrapped, but the tree still lay horizontally on the front lawn. Mum wanted us to put it up and my brother and I wanted to go duck shooting. Having agreed to return in good time and promised faithfully to have the tree up and decorated before Church, we strode out along the valley. The old oak trees that stand on the bank above the pond showed clearly at first against the bright sky but, as the clouds raced in, they faded rapidly into the wood behind. The rain came first, with a biting wind that stung the face. As we turned for home after a fruitless wait, flecks of white moved among the raindrops, increasing till the air was full of driving snow.

In the ten minutes it took us to walk home, the ground had turned white, and so had the still-horizontal Christmas tree. That the tree was erected, decorated and Church attended was testament to feverish endeavour and the conviction that the carpet would dry before morning. I still dream of a white Christmas and the symbolic power it can have over man and commercialisation.

10

CHAPTER TEN

The vacuum that follows Christmas is sometimes called the January blues. Christmas is barely out, and the head barely cleared, before the children are back to school and the house begins to rattle. In many ways, this is the ideal time for a farmer - and especially a sheep and Bed and Breakfasting farmer - to get away. Skiing was a great favourite till Chris hurt her knee, and now far-off sunny climes certainly looked inviting and were, in many ways, needed. But no, this year we would stay at home. School fees plus new roof did not add up to holidays, even in my elementary mathematics. We would busy ourselves with some light decorating and enjoy the challenge the New Year would hold.

The kitchen had already been declared a priority zone and had been started before Christmas as part of our ongoing campaign to shake ourselves into action. It had become obvious at about the same time, that no one was having a New Year's Eve Party, or at least no one was inviting us. We rang round and found that this was the year when everyone was leaving the party organising to everyone else. Some years there seem to be hundreds of parties and you end up drifting around several on a pint of orange juice or staying at one and risking offending the rest. But there must be a party at the New Year, we decided. It would be here, and we started inviting.

As with many farmers, I met my wife at the local Young Farmers Club. By the time we married I had run the gauntlet of Club Chairman and was about to be County Chairman. Chris had belonged to a club at the other end of the county and we had done our bit for inter-club relations. Partying and Young Farmers are synonymous, and the huge cellar which runs the full length of the large Sitting Room had become associated with New Year revelry. After we became too old for Young Farmers, the cellar had reverted to its former use as a store and games room.

The next generation of Young Farmers had discovered that we had moved back to the farmhouse and approached us with: 'Can we have a cellar party? Half the club are going with the neighbouring club to dance in the fountains at Trafalgar Square, so we won't be many.'

We thought about their request, of our fond memories of such events only a few years before, and of how it would clash with our own party. We decided to compromise.

'You can have the cellar and the kitchen, which we are half-way to decorating. We will have the large Sitting Room and Breakfast Room. We will come and dance with you in the cellar.'

'Fine', they agreed, 'but may we charge our friends a pound entrance fee to cover food costs?'

'Okay, but make sure you don't charge our guests.'

With a friendly gibe about our friends being too old to be mistaken for Young Farmers, we went our own ways to start organising.

It's funny how fog can come down when it is least wanted. Apparently, even intrepid Young Farmers don't travel in fog anymore and, when the coach trip they had organised was called off, we were destined for an eventful evening.

All seemed to start well; our guests were politely shown to the warm and comfortable Sitting Room, while the Young Farmers descended into the bowels of the earth. Yes, there seemed plenty of them, but they were tolerably well-behaved and the vaulting and soil filling that separates the Sitting Room from the cellar below was a superb sound barrier. Several guests commented that the cellar had a good atmosphere and seemed fairly full, but it wasn't until we discovered that they had taken over £150 that we realised there must have been nearly two hundred and fifty people in the house that night. Fortunately, the farmyard gave adequate car parking and the loo system held out.

It was a tribute to the old house that such an event was enjoyed by all and that the high walls retained enough sound for the neighbours to sleep - those that hadn't come, that is. The next morning, the Young Farmers arrived in force and cleared everything away. Conversation was minimal, but then I wasn't very talkative either.

After they had gone, I stood alone in the old cellar. It is considered by many to be much older than the house and probably belonged to a previous property that had been burnt down or demolished. It is totally self-supporting, with a full arched vault spanning the room till about five feet from the ground. The walls are of local stone and roughhewn. The entrance steps are also of stone, deeply worn and leading from a side chamber into the middle of the cellar itself. As it enters the main cellar, the entrance cuts a deep, vaulted groove at right angles to the main vault and is mirrored on the far side by a vault that leads to the breather in the garden outside. To the left is a row of stone benching, originally for holding cider or beer barrels, and the floor slopes gradually throughout, to a drain in the centre. The benching is now seating, and the drain covered. When decked for a party, the lights cascade along the vaulting, creating a mosaic of light and shadow in the rough stone. In the old party days, rows of cushions would follow the low walls and the atmosphere, when occupied by seventy teenagers, was electric.

She had blonde hair, which shone orange in the flashing lights. Her face looked pale but from it appeared two large eyes. She was sitting in the corner, uneasily trying to ignore the couple on her right. She was happy to escape, to come for the dance. The rough stone floor was unsafe for vigorous dancing, the ceiling low at the sides, the dozens of people. We smooched.

'Where are you from?', I seemed to shout as the music lulled.

'Islip', I heard her reply. I think her name was Julie - or was it Judy? It doesn't matter now. Memories are what matter and mine are of those gently sexy eyes, shining from the face with the orange hair. Many years on, I try to remember the feeling that came welling in me then, but it is gone. I am left with a deep fondness for the atmosphere of this wonderful room and wonder what the children will make of it when their time comes.

~~~~~~~~~~~~~~~~~~~

James had gone to boarding school with a deep, basic love of sport. As with many small County Primary Schools his introduction to it had been basic in the extreme. The fact that he had been in a year with three girls to every boy hadn't helped. I have a love of cricket, stemming back to when my grandfather would take me to watch Oxford University in the Parks, and sometimes to Worcester. One of the joys of youth was to be driven down the Woodstock Road in Oxford in early summer, the cherry blossom cascading from mature trees that lined the road, the glorious scent carried in the gentle breeze and the thoughts of the match to come.

I am lucky that James seems to have inherited this enthusiasm and soon learnt to bowl and hit the ball. He has always been a strong and thick-set lad, and playing mini-rugby at the local club soon became a regular Sunday morning outing. I was amazed how such young lads - he started playing for the under eights - could take such crunching and obviously painful tackles, which, if suffered at home, would have required immediate treatment and sympathy, but here needed only a momentary grimace and then back to the scrum. If, after the match, I enquired as to how the sore leg felt, I would receive a long-bewildered look and the comment, 'What sore leg?'

His first term at boarding school had been a great success, especially after he gained his place in one of the school teams. He was lucky to have Mick Norman as his coach, a great ex-Leicestershire and Northampton opening batsman, who views correct technique as vital. His rapport with the boys brings out the best in them, and the team spirit, love of the game and desire to constantly improve on what he has instilled, is something for which I will be eternally grateful.

The autumn term had been rugby and, as James's game improved, so did his work. His dyslexia would be something he would have to live with and work hard to overcome; this he was doing and with so much joy and confidence. Several talks with his form master had convinced me that his success on the sports field was being mirrored by his success in the classroom. He would never be scholastically intellectual, but his improvement in the class had been sound.

So, as he returned in January, we were particularly apprehensive. This was to be the hockey term, a game he had never played and for which his experience at the base of the scrum seemed most inappropriate. We need not have worried. Although he did not instantly shine, he showed surprising agility and control, to which he added the desire to work at this new challenge. After all, sport is sport.

Undoubtedly, the most memorable incident regarding hockey occurred three years later. James had passed his common entrance and was now at Rugby. Sport was still the fulcrum around which the world rotated and it was now the turn of hockey, a sport with which the school was particularly well endowed that year, with many county and area players and even an international. Chris had been preparing James for a term in the second or lower team for his age.

'We will support you, whichever team you are in, and if you work at it, who knows?'

He listened, with a grin that was part wicked and part condescending. Shortly after the term had begun, we received the term calendar and looked at the fixture list.

'If he managed the seconds he would be away at Cheltenham', Chris said, still reading. 'I'll write and tell him we'll go and watch, it may encourage him.'

The match was to be played on the Saturday and, on the Friday evening, the phone rang. It was James, his voice seemed low and tired.

'I'm not playing at Cheltenham, Mum', he said, and waited for a reply. Chris passed on the message to me as I sat in the chair.

'Never mind, keep trying. Have you a match at all?'

'Oh yes, we have a game here, but I wouldn't bother to come.'

This was like a red rag to a bull and Chris leapt at it with a determination based on sympathy.

'Where will you be playing, on one of the practice pitches?'

'No.'

'Then where?', said Chris, with growing concern.

'On the AstroTurf.'

'Why the AstroTurf?'

'Well, the firsts always play on the AstroTurf.'

He wisely rang off before the flood of pride, mixed with fury at being conned for unjustified sympathy, reverberated down the line.

~~~~~~~~~~~~~~~~~~

As the new year got underway, our thoughts concentrated on the challenges this next twelve months held in store. We had only been doing

Bed and Breakfast for a year, yet it had changed our lives. The balance of farming and Bed and Breakfast, with the potential of hospitality days and fly fishing on the lake, all came into the reckoning. The economic recession was beginning to rear its head, especially in farming, and the recent drought summer, whilst encouraging paying guests, had played havoc with the crops. Most importantly, our reaction to filling the house with potential strangers had been pleasantly reassuring. We had always liked people, but the thoughts of our fist visitors were warm and happy. They had enriched our lives and we had genuinely enjoyed having them. With this confident base, we set about organising ourselves to maximise the house and the lake, and prepare for the sheep sale in October. We could already picture the new roof making next winter a warmer time; our goal seemed straight ahead.

But how to bring this happy house and beautiful lake, bubbling with trout, to the notice of those with money to spend? The Bed and Breakfast was already advertised with the Tourist Board, as well as with an agency and in travel books. The main Oxford to Stratford road runs less than a mile away and thoughts of a well-designed road sign to show travellers of our existence seemed an obvious extension. We would write to the council. The fishing and hospitality days seemed more of a problem. The fishing could be advertised in magazines and by a mail shot, but what of the hospitality days?

'You need a good brochure', said Harry, over a drink one Sunday morning. 'Some good photos showing what you can do, well set out, with a brief description. A glossy finish would add a bit of class, make it look more professional. I could take the photos and Helen in the office will do the rest. She's very good.'

It was agreed before Harry left the house and the next week I went to see Helen. Harry came out to take some pictures of a friend in full fishing gear, with my father acting as gillie. The fact that neither knew a fish from a tadpole was irrelevant. A shot of clay pigeons being flung off our steep banks with the valley stretching far below formed the front cover, and there was a view of the house with a fish net in the foreground and more people with horses beyond.

'What about food?', said Harry, knowing that Chris was a good cook and had catered for his Vintage Austin Club. Before she could answer, he rushed on, 'How about a dinner party in your big Sitting Room with the fire roaring in the background?'

Chris waited for him to take a breath and jumped in.

'Fine, I will invite the guests and you bring Helen and take the photos. Which night do you want it?', reaching for her diary.

The big room certainly makes an attractive dining room, the long table bedecked in its finery, the candles glowing brightly in the gentle light, long green curtains, flashes of brightness on silver and mirrors, and the fire, reigning supreme beyond, a king on his throne.

The first guests arrived and moved into the Breakfast Room, acting as a sitting room for the occasion, and within a few minutes all were present, except Harry and his wife, Helen. Two Helens in an increasingly complicated plot! Another drink was served and conversation continued. Eventually they arrived, flustered and muttering about babysitters.

Some couples can feel annoyed with each other, or the world, or both, but not show it openly or immediately. Bottled up, however, the hidden annoyance can wait for an appropriate or even inappropriate moment to appear, not unlike the top coming off an over-reactive bottle of homemade beer. Little did we know that tonight was going to be one of over-fermentation.

The food had been put on hold and was now being brought to readiness as Harry entered the kitchen. I had been sent to start the procession into the dining room and show everyone to their allotted place. The concern over Harry's late arrival was melting as the drink flowed. Laughter increasingly broke the surface, like a long-watched pot coming to the boil and gently simmering. In the kitchen things were about to get even hotter.

'I'm going home', said Harry, stopping Chris as she stirred a sauce.

'But you can't, the dinner's ready and this evening is for the photos.' Harry wasn't listening.

'I must go, the babysitter needs relieving.'

'Don't be silly, Ben is only a few weeks old and Helen is feeding him herself. Sit down and have another drink.'

Harry rose and made to leave, but Chris took the car keys deftly from his hand.

'If you go, you can walk, Helen will need the car later.' She thought of mentioning the photos again, but knew this had nothing to do with either the photos or the dinner - but what, and why now?

While Chris was busy in the kitchen, I was doing my Fawlty Towers bit, reassuring guests that all would be well, as the principal walked the two miles home. Leonard, our young vicar, was summoned from the table and drove off to recover Harry and the situation. The first course, long delayed, was served. The saga of the kitchen came out to raucous laughter and the meal was saved. All we needed was a photographer. He finally came, having almost reached home before being pacified and retrieved by Leonard.

The photos came out well, obviously some passion remained in dear Harry. True to form, he was back to his outrageous best by the end of the evening. It is an evening that will always come back to me in vivid detail every time I show someone the brochure. They probably wonder why I break into an unlikely grin, but could never know the answer.

Within a week, every sign of a grin had been wiped from my face. A tooth, which had felt a little tender when I went to bed, woke me with a vengeance in the early hours and refused to listen to even a surfeit of paracetamol. I struggled through till breakfast and then contacted my dentist.

Ali is not your typical dentist. With bright, expressive eyes, blonde hair and curves where every girl dreams of having them, she helped dull the pain immediately. I had first met her at a party, bubbly, witty, flashes of joy in a dull evening. The next day, I became her patient. Tipped back in the chair, I looked at her, those same eyes peering from behind a paper mask. She peeled it back.

'Bob, I thought your eyes were only like that when you were drunk.'

It was just my luck that, as my tooth raged, she was away for the day. Her assistant would have to do. Noreen is very petite and certainly means well, but looked terribly small compared to the pain I was asking her to remove. It would have to come out, she decided, after an eternity of prodding. Why is a dental syringe so huge when your mouth is rivetted in pain and can only be opened a centimetre? Whether it was caused by the sight of the scalpel and nutcracker in hand, or the determination on her face akin to a weightlifter going for a record and hitherto impossible lift, a light terror grew within me. Time drifted, like fog under a neon streetlight, heavy and depressed, swirled occasionally by an invisible hand. She stood as tall as her four-foot-two would allow and exerted all her effort but, gradually, the fact that the tooth was the stronger became apparent as the pain returned.

'No, it won't move. You'll have to come back tomorrow when Ali is here. It might throb a bit later', and she shrugged her exhausted shoulders and turned away.

Although the pain echoed with every heartbeat, I felt a strange pride in this wretched tooth. It had served me well for many years and it obviously didn't want to leave me now. But, within an hour, any sentimental attachment to the tooth had gone. It was slightly loose and my tongue could not resist exploring this strange phenomenon in its midst.

The phone rang. Ali was back from her meeting and full of concern for my condition. She would be out in two hours to finish the job. I felt like a leaking pipe that continually frustrated the plumber. A few minutes later, my thoughts became more akin to those of a stage actor, as several friends and neighbours, having heard that my pretty dentist was making a rare house visit, decided to come and watch the tragedy unfold.

The small sitting room was more intimate and would give them all a decent view. Ali has that quality, found in many successful women, that tells you anything is possible. So, when she strained to exert pressure on the re-numbed thing that was a tooth, I felt an ominous confidence that it would soon be over. The cracking sound echoed like a gun in my head and had obviously been impressive to the assembled gathering. As I opened my eyes, they were all murmuring to each other. I was glad they were getting their money's worth. Ali stood with a resigned smile, her eyes lifted from the tooth she held in front of her, and turned to me.

'I'm afraid it's snapped off. I can't inject you any more now, come back in the morning and I'll drill out the root.'

Ali went to talk to Chris and the audience enquired about tickets for the replay. Tomorrow came and went with snatches of memory. More injections, probing and drilling and, when it was over, total exhaustion. It certainly reaffirmed my view that teeth were one of the Almighty's lesser creations. I looked up.

'Lord, you could have done a lot better with a bit more effort.'

Every couple of years, Ali goes to Israel for a fortnight in the early spring, doing charity dentist work. Most of the participants in the scheme are married and take their families. As Ali was still single, she offered to take Chris. It was too good a chance to miss. Her love of the sun had been thwarted by my ability to turn into a lobster after five minutes. The girls got on well and, as they boarded the plane, I was sure they would have a great time.

The two weeks she was away were taken up with caring for sheep and guests. The latter included a beautiful French girl called Nicole, who was just a couple of years younger than me. Her children, in their early teens, were attending a language school in Oxford, and she decided to hover nearby to be on hand if needed and to enjoy herself if not. She taught English as a foreign language and accompanied me on two visits to James and Vicki's schools to see dramatic productions. I enjoyed her company, her wit, her French elegance and it certainly did my street cred some good as the gossip flooded the village.

The few days between Nicole's departure and Chris's return gave me the chance to prove my bachelor status. During the fortnight, many friends had invited me to supper or lunch, taking pity on a poor, deserted husband. Now was my chance to prove my culinary ability. I invited a dozen to supper and set to planning my menu. I decided to start with choux pastry filled with paté, move on to colonial goose and finish with grapes soaked in whisky. The starter I could do early on the morning of the supper, the grapes would need to be done a couple of days before and the goose, what about the goose? As you may know, a colonial goose is not a bird at all, but a leg of lamb, boned and stuffed with oatmeal, apricots and honey. I had heard of the recipe some time ago, but never tried it, nor had I ever boned a leg of lamb. Indeed, my memory of chasing the apparently reanimated limb around the kitchen will last long in my memory!

As the evening approached, the preparations had gone worryingly well. The starter looked incredibly like the picture in the cookbook and, when filled with my special tuna-based concoction, seemed very edible. I prepared some tomatoes for colour and slid the dish into the fridge. The grapes peered at me through their cling-film cover and, when I peeled back a corner, gave off an aroma I thought very suitable for the expected party.

I turned to the goose. The gladiatorial contest the previous evening had been declared a draw although, as I took it from the fridge, I claimed a moral victory. I hoped the dish I was about to retrieve would look, feel, and smell as the book had claimed and the glossy picture showed. That it looked more like an overfat haggis was a great disappointment. The stitches that held it together and were needed to retain the apricots and honey looked very uneven, and would they survive the cooking? Anyway, this was a time for action and so, fortified by the glass of red wine that all television chefs seem to live on, I fed the object into the oven and went upstairs to change. I could lay the table later.

As I started the impossible hunt for an ironed shirt, after nearly two weeks of bachelorhood, the potential for disaster crept over me. I felt happy in my meal preparation, worryingly so. I began to worry about my happiness when so much could go wrong. 'You have no right to feel so confident.' 'Why', I countered, 'I am merely reciprocating the relaxed hospitality of good friends. If the dishes, the ideas, the flavours work, so be it; if they don't, we can all have a good laugh.' 'Fine' I heard my other self reply, 'if you really believe that'. This had the potential for deep self analysis but was cut short by the first car drawing into the drive, and with the table still unlaid.

I am sure wives need to feel that both their husbands and other wives' husbands are basically inept in kitchens. Few wives would challenge the organisation for a meal prepared by a fellow wife. They may comment, even bitchily, to other girls later about this or that but, on the day, politeness and respect for another wife's territory would reign. Arrival would be slightly late to allow for corrections to any unforeseen disasters, and any unwanted smell of burning would be totally ignored.

My first guests arrived fifteen minutes early. They seemed unable to accept my casual approach to time and preparation and, breezing through into the kitchen, started to help. By help, I do, of course, mean take over. They dashed here and there as if nothing had been prepared at all, with the occasional smile, chuckle and 'you've done very well really.' I was thus truly pleased when the starter seemed genuinely appreciated and plates emptied. I took the goose from the oven to find it intact and golden. Some of the honey had escaped and now glistened appetizingly.

It still looked like a pregnant haggis, but at least an edible haggis. The effect upon carving was one of silence.

Initially I was uncertain, were they impressed or just bewildered? Were they feasting with admiration or trying to decipher its identity? I decided silence to be the best policy.

'Is that honey?', asked Lynn, breaking the void as she leant over and dipped her finger into the juice.

'Yes, among other things', I replied, wanting to maintain the mystery and teasing her into guessing what they were. Ann, used to more formal occasions, finally succumbed to the need to finger dip.

'Apricots!', she exclaimed. I smiled confirmation and decided it was time to carve.

The meat folded back to reveal apricots and oatmeal, shining and dripping with honey. The effect was wonderful. The girls had a look of amazement, mixed with admiration. They wanted to know, how had I made it and in what proportions, as they bent over the table to give it a prod. They turned to their men with the, 'why can't you do that?' look, and returned to eating. The men gave me the expected 'you traitor' look, but seemed to enjoy the meal. The lasting effect was that bachelor times resulted in far less sympathy and fewer invitations out. But, as I bid the last guest goodnight and started to clear the empty dishes, I felt an inner glow of success.

11

CHAPTER ELEVEN

These early-year distractions had allowed the approach of summer and the need to make preparations for the sale drift by almost unnoticed. Chris's fortnight away had given me ample practice at making breakfast and spending a quiet hour, pen and paper in hand, putting together a schedule for the sale. The details for the catalogue would not be needed for a couple of months yet but, as we had already committed ourselves as to numbers of sheep and their ages, it was vital that they grew and improved to look their best on the day. The marquee had to be booked, caterers arranged and advertising organised.

Whilst this went on, more immediately pressing matters loomed large. I have mentioned our previous early-year outings to the Bath and West show at Shepton Mallet, and Newark for the Newark and Notts, taking in the two May Bank Holiday weekends. It had been decided that, in order to publicise our forthcoming on-farm sale, we should, once again, have a presence at these events. The show at Newark came first, with the show at Shepton Mallet at the end of the month. This latter event we saw as a chance to send some butcher's lambs. This used to be a regular for us and I was keen to see if our stock could still receive the plaudits we had in the past. That we won both the heavy and light sections and came away with the champion's cup was beyond my wildest dreams. We made sure the press covered it well, with photos where it mattered and mention of the October sale clearly stated.

Yet, it had been the event at Newark early in the month that really mattered. Having the best carcass is one thing, and it would be well noticed by commercial ram buyers; but pedigree buyers, which would be to the fore in October, wanted to see our pure stock be successful too. Now we needed to produce the real thing!

The show had many sections for the Texel breed based on gender and age, starting with the young ewe lambs and ending with the older rams. We hadn't entered a ewe lamb, deciding ours would be smaller than many and not wanting to be beaten. The yearling ewe class came next and I was not looking forward to it. Our chosen sheep had come down lame just before the show and I wasn't confident about its replacement. I watched as it rested in its pen prior to judging and couldn't resist looking at the larger sheep in the next pen. The steward called us forward and, having carefully fitted the halter to my nervous sheep, entered the ring.

Sheep, as people, can react to different situations in different ways. Some people love to perform in public, they love to have an audience, while others feel embarrassed and shy away. This hitherto unremarkable animal suddenly blossomed. She seemed far larger than she had in her pen and demanded the judge's attention. If his gaze drifted to any other sheep she bleated loudly, as if to say, 'You don't need to waste your time looking over there, just look at me.' She won the class, there could be no other verdict and our day went forward from there. She also won the best of breed prize and now stood in the interbreed championship. This class is very difficult, and the breed from which the judge is selected often feel confident. In this case, they were so confident they had already put their champagne on ice. Something that made the victory of our sheep all the more pleasurable and set us up perfectly to advertise the sale.

As the weeks slipped by and more breeders admired my courage at putting so many eggs into one basket, I tried not to dwell on the consequences of failure. The whole ram sale season would have come and gone by then and, for now, that was distraction enough. The lambs had just been weaned from their mothers and moved on to a crop of oats and vetches. This historic blend of the pea-like vetch and stout oat to hold it up, has been grown here for generations. Best planted in the autumn, it gives good grazing over several weeks during the dry part of mid-summer, when the grass is getting stemmy and old. The lambs are given as much as they can eat every day and slowly move, nomad like, across the field. The vetches give luxurious growth, crowned with a beautiful purple flower. The oats stand tall and erect, waving their bells of heavy grains in the breeze, as guardians keeping watch.

There is little feed value in the oats, much more in the vetches, but together they complement each other. They look so timeless; I think of my grandfather's tale of the shepherd leaning on the gate.

'Have you no work, Jones?', the farmer demands, on seeing his employee apparently idle.

'Oh yes, sir, I'm very busy doing the most important job.'

'Busy doing what?', the farmer replies.

'Busy observing your sheep, sir', the shepherd answers.

I have spent many minutes observing my sheep, as they move across an area of new oats and vetches. They will walk a yard or two, sniffing here and there, perhaps having a taste here, then a nibble there, before suddenly taking a huge mouthful of green oat grains or a certain plant of vetch. Several rapid mouthfuls, enough to choke, too much to swallow, some falling to the ground, wasted, others moving on with a quick swallow, a deep breath and another turn of the cycle. The sound of a flock of sheep, all in their own eating cycles, all with their own variation on the theme, gels together into one of the most relaxing and contented sounds I know.

A few weeks after the lambs have settled into their new paradise, the yearling rams are moved on to the crop alongside them. These rams were too young to sell as lambs and are now being prepared for sale at about eighteen months of age. At this time, the rams are growing well, putting on more weight, size and wool, and definitely dislike hot, airless weather. Shade is important and any well-placed tree or high hedge becomes populated by wall-to-wall resting sheep during the heat of the day.

It was during one of those dry, airless passages of early summer, when all normal people lie down in the cool, that we prepared to go to a summer ball. We had arranged a party of twelve, a friend's safari Land Rover had been borrowed, so we only needed one driver, and a feeling of calm and opulence was descending on us. The ladies looked radiant in their ball gowns, flowing with mixes of bright summer colours. The men dulled in their dinner suites but looked tall and dignified, like the oats in the field beyond. Chris had mixed some Pimm's in the big Sitting Room, cooled by the thick walls of the old house, with flashes of sun breaking through the vine leaves that covered the windows. The doorbell rang; four tired Belgian girls had reached their accommodation. Chris hurried past.

'Yes, hello, I'm Chris and we're expecting you, please come through.'

As she ushered them past the assembly, towards their rooms, a look of impressed bewilderment hung on their faces. They were on a tour of England and this was their first night. As they joined us for a glass of Pimm's, their impression of life on an English farm was already filling with misconception.

The ball was truly superb, the old hall proving an ideal setting, opening onto well-manicured lawns and glorious views beyond. The food was wonderfully presented, cold meats and leaping salmon on water-like mirrored dishes.

I think it was a prawn that started my downfall that evening. By the sweet, a feeling of unsteadiness had been joined by one of inner insecurity. I went for a well-timed walk, but could not rouse the desire for company or food. I slipped away and found somewhere to lie down. I felt slightly better when the sound of starting engines and loud laughter woke me. There can be little worse than the witty humour of alcoholic friends in the confines of a safari Land Rover, when you are both very sober and decidedly unwell. Chris is best described as a flamboyant driver and I did not need flamboyance.

Philip, always a mine of jokes and seated opposite me in the rear of the vehicle, became the focus of attention. His jokes were long and well developed, with many pauses for the depth of situations to sink home, all delivered in the appropriate voice.

'A gentleman visited a stately home as an overnight guest but arrived too late to be shown anything but his room. He soon realised he needed the bathroom and crept into the corridor.' Philip waited for the predicament to register. Chris lurched through a pothole and I held my breath.

'He dared not try the doors, lest they led to a lady's bedroom and ensuing embarrassment, so he went downstairs, thinking to use the garden, but the front door was locked.' Again, a wait for the company to envisage the gentleman's position. I closed my eyes, but that didn't help either.

'In desperation, he noticed a large urn, which topped a low pillar at the bottom of the grand staircase. A few minutes later, he was back in bed and feeling much better. As he left the next morning, a distinctly unpleasant smell was now spreading across the hall and, when he arrived home later in the day, a telegram was waiting. It said, 'Know it was you, but where?''

Some of the group had followed it through and laughed spontaneously, others had dozed but, when woken by the laughter, joined in. The best I dared manage was a pained smile.

Chris has always upheld that the only way to conclude a ball is to finish with breakfast in the early hours, when the only dish should be kippers. The breakfast room table had been laid with all its finery, ready for our return. Two high pedestals with cascades of flowers had been acquired at the ball, and soon stood almost to the ceiling at each end of the table. The effect was stunning, but so was the thought of kippers on my still-complaining stomach and I crept away. Fully dressed in my dining suit, I collapsed onto my bed and slept.

I dimly recollect Chris joining me shortly before I woke fully. I looked at the clock, saw it showed six-thirty, and sat up with a start. I had suddenly remembered that the Belgian girls wanted breakfast at seven. One look at Chris told me she would not be in a breakfast-cooking condition in half an hour. I rose to my feet and felt surprisingly stable. I threw some cold water over my face in an attempt to wipe last night from my mind and encourage it to enter today, decided I didn't have time to change and hurried downstairs. Spurred on by the sounds of movement from the girls' rooms, I quickly re-laid the table, looking the other way as I cleared the remains of the kippers.

The memory of cold fish still rang alarm bells in my brain and brought sympathy movements from my stomach. I had just completed the preparations and run a comb through my hair, when the girls entered and the cooking of breakfast, which I can now do on automatic pilot, began. I felt quietly pleased with myself as they finished their meals and went upstairs to get ready for their bus. I sat at the table pondering over a cup of tea and looking about me. The flowers still hung from their pedestals and showed little wear, for all their exploits. The tablecloth was still fairly clean and the unused glasses still stood on the dresser in the corner. It must have been a strange sight to have been served breakfast here by an unsteady young man in his dinner jacket. But for them, of course, this was their first breakfast in England, and they may have seen nothing strange in it. There can be no doubt that, wherever they took breakfast tomorrow, it would not be the same.

~~~~~~~~~~~~~~~~~

This was one of my favourite times by the lake. Now three years old, the vegetation had achieved amazing maturity and with it had grown the richness and diversity of the bird and insect life. Eighteen months before, we had stocked it with a mix of brown and rainbow trout. The brown trout is the native of the Glyme and is a fish of great dignity and even greater difficulty to catch in the crystal-clear waters. The rainbow, although less attractive, prefers lakes, grows faster and is easier to catch. As we were intending to develop the lake as a fishery, it was vital that some fish were catchable, even by the most inexperienced or inept angler.

We had started fishing in May by inviting friends and acquaintances and, by June, were confident that the fish in the lake had not only survived but also grown well and were in excellent health. A local feed firm had shown interest in holding a barbeque with us and the rep's car was parked in the drive when I returned to the house after a very enjoyable walk around the stock. The walk had taken me round the lake, as the sun rose above the steep valley sides and cast its ripples of brightness across the water. Fish had been rising for flies and, as this extra light and warmth aroused the insect life into action, the lake took on the appearance of a pot coming to the boil. Nestled in a pocket of the valley, the lake is protected from outside sounds, and the seclusion acts to increase the importance of its own life. I entered the house in a rejuvenated mood and joined Chris and Andy for a cup of coffee.

Andy's humour had developed well in the few months we had known him. A sales rep calling on farmers must have a sense of humour or his life will be made impossible. He must learn to laugh at himself and we had assumed the responsibility of developing this for him.

'Selling some more cut-price cow cake?', I smiled as I looked round the door, knowing that he had really come for payment for the sheep feed we had bought the previous month.

'You need more customers and the way to do that is to look after the ones you have already.' Andy looked suspicious, wondered what sarcasm would come next.

'Entertainment.' I paused, he still looked doubtful. 'You must entertain your regular customers, let them spread the word. That's the way to draw more trade.'

He still looked doubtful but understanding developed in his face. He began to realise it to be a genuine suggestion, rather than a poor joke at his expense. Conversation moved from feeds to food and to barbeque, whereupon I added the fishy ingredient. Why not have a fishing evening with the barbeque? The lakeside at dusk is the ultimate venue and fishing would give it more appeal and excitement. I felt the salesman in me coming to the surface, as I let the emotions that my recent walk had aroused come out like a child after his first day at the beach. Like all good reps, Andy listened with mock appreciation, gave no commitment and said he would pass on the idea.

After he had gone, we worked out the logistics of doing a barbeque by the lake. It would mean moving all the equipment and would depend on the weather but, with the excitement that a new idea brings and the reassurance that something could be done in the big Sitting Room if it was wet, we persevered. The area chief phoned several days later. Andy had mentioned the fishing to him and, as a fisherman himself, he wanted to see the lake. He arrived that evening complete with rod and, when he caught a beautiful two-pound rainbow with his third cast, I knew we were in business.

Back in the house, we discussed numbers and menus, all-in prices and use of equipment, and finished up with a booking for twenty. As the day neared, I became more confident about our plans for the barbeque and the weather forecast seemed set fair, but what about the little fishes?

What if none chose to bite, if the number of fishermen proved too great and the evening as a fishing experience proved a flop? I turned over in bed to let the worry dissolve. I wonder if fashion designers have this same kind of worry before the first review of their new exhibition.

'The best contacts are personal contacts' rolled over in my mind. Yes, and the worst are dissatisfied customers. How many potential fishermen and friends of fishermen would we lose when, after several hours' effort, they went home with no fish?

I walked around the lake on the morning, before the breeze woke the water. I checked the barbeque site and measured the car park. The grass had been topped the previous day and the sweet smell hung in the air. 'All will be well if you play your part, fishes', I spoke out loud, looking searchingly into the water.

John arrived with his car bulging with prizes for the strange competitions, from 'ugliest fish' to the more predictable 'most fish caught'. As he unloaded these and followed with his huge array of fishing equipment, my meagre confidence started to flow from me, as water from a holey bucket. I directed myself to arranging the tables by the barbeque and setting out some bales to act as seating. Guests started arriving in that unlikely mix of vehicles, which is somehow only identifiable with a gathering of farmers. New Daihatsus and old Minis in an equally identifiable parking chaos that uses anything but a line.

The lake had been constructed so one side had no obstructions behind for at least fifty yards and, as the first fisherman started casting under John's watchful eye, I knew we would need every inch of it. Some were experienced fishermen, whose deft touch could send a fly tens of yards over the water to land like a feather directly over a rising fish. Others would watch this but try to use force in lieu of timing. Their line would judder a few yards and land with a splash, causing ripples of water as well as laughter across the lake. Fortunately, the first fish was soon breaking the surface, the tempo of the evening rose and an air of friendly competition took over.

Some I knew, sheep or cattle farmers from the area; some, such as Paul, had bought rams from me. Others I had shot with, a few were vague market acquaintances, the rest total strangers. Together, they were a party, here for a good time.

We stopped after a couple of hours for food. Steak and kebabs, lamb sausages and pork chops, jacket potatoes and an array of salads that only a summer's evening can provide. No one was in a hurry as the sun set up the valley. Two ducks landed on the lake, undaunted by the lights or the fire, and bats buzzed over the water. Fish rise to take flies moving on the surface of the water and, as these flies can vary with the smallest change of wind or temperature, a rise of fish is often not consistent and certainly not predictable. The quiet of the immediate pre-food period was broken by the steadily increasing activity of fishermen eating. As the fish rose more, so a haste was visible on the faces of the diners. Anxiety not to miss their chance was tempered by the desire to eat all their food.

Peter, fishing on the narrow side of the lake, came from a long line of sporting farmers. His prowess at shooting I had witnessed first-hand some years ago and now I stood in awe as, with barely any movement of the wrist or arm, his line would arch in slow, controlled sweeps before dropping with absolute precision. Within minutes, his first fish was landed. Around the lake, more and more fishermen were using him as a textbook. Retrieving their line from a reed bed or thistle clump, they would look across at Peter as a cook might study the picture in a new recipe book.

Martin was an acknowledged farmer and improving shot. His physique was that of a second row forward and, when he stood by the lake with a rod borrowed from his grandfather, it was a scene of comedy. If Peter's casting technique was a thing of poetry, Martin's was best likened to a shot-put on a string, or perhaps welly throwing.

'Are you using a dry fly?', David shouted across the water. Martin, on the far bank, pulled in his line and looked at the end, a ball of soggy fluff.

'It looks pretty wet to me', he replied, to the mirth of more experienced fisherman. It became as important to help the novices make their first catch as it was for the more experienced to catch the big fish to win the prize.

In dry fly fishing it is important to keep the fly as dry as possible, so that it floats naturally on the surface film of the water. Martin's would break this film like a brick thrown from Tower Bridge; consequently, he would spend as long drying his fly as actually fishing. He treated this unique experience with stoic good humour; showing real elation if the fly landed anywhere near its target.

If Martin had actually caught a fish, it would have been the sensation of the evening. That he didn't showed that reality will invariably win over romance. Another glance across to Peter brought hope. The reality of his success was plain for all to see, yet the artistry that brought this success was truly romantic. If evidence were needed that fishing can be aesthetic and an art form, rather than applied science, the last light on the lake was witness to it.

As the evening drew to a close, many fish had been caught and a three-pounder from Peter was favourite for the prize. George returned from where the water flowed from the lake back into the river.

'I wish I had brought my spinner', he said. 'There's a nice pike in the river below the lake.' I wandered round, collecting my snare from its place behind the old willow tree. A few minutes later I returned with a four-pound pike thrashing at the end of the wire.

'I think this must win the prize', I proclaimed, with mock sincerity.

~~~~~~~~~~~~~~~~~~~

The full blaze of early summer was bursting from every tree, the spring sowing was complete and promise becoming realised in the long rows of vibrant young plants. The lambing was long-since over and lambing yards cleaned and empty, and, as I finished planting the cover crops, my thoughts turned to winter.

Just as now is a time of increasing plenty, so winter can be one of cold, exposure and hunger, as a fresh, cold north wind funnels up the valley or rakes the top land. The wildlife, so encouraged by the increased habitat by the lake and the new tree plantings up the valley, would soon perish unless provision was made now for those bleak, far-off winter times. Small cover crops of kale and maize are planted in half-acre blocks about the farm, giving security when even the turnips prove inadequate. Unnecessary as this might seem now, it means that a stealthy approach on a snowy morning in January will result in an explosion, not just of pheasant and partridge, but of every common songbird the area possesses. Soon, migratory visitors will appear to join the throng. Anyone who can stand in the warm comfort of their home and condemn country sports should see this scene. They might appreciate how the feed crops, paid for by shooting and hunting, give infinitely more life than they threaten and are part of a planned progression that gives us the most concentrated and diverse wildlife of any country in Europe.

That the public are only able to witness this from footpaths, which a very small minority use, or from the road, along which most travel at such speed that the only knowledge of local wildlife is likely to have a certain fatality about it, is very sad. With this in mind, I decided to give a conducted tour of the farm. I posted a note on the village noticeboard and broadcast the event in the parish magazine. I decided on seven o'clock as a good meeting time. Ample opportunity for people to return from the office and grab a bit of tea, and still enough light to circumnavigate the farm aboard a tractor and trailer, taking in the delights of the estate. I was naive enough to believe that people actually wanted to know how crops were grown; how modern farming was wearing a caring face, planting trees and leaving wild, watery areas. I should have been pleased that six people turned their backs on an evening's television and mounted the trailer that evening, but I wasn't.

Stopping at regular intervals along the way, I gave a full account of cropping procedures and rotations, explaining the attempt to marry profitable modern farming with my custodial duties. The lake looked long and exciting from the top of the hill, its ripples shining through the tall willow, which flashed light and dark greens in the evening breeze. I felt proud that evening, the blend of necessary efficiency and natural untidiness was about right. Few felt the feelings that were behind my explanations; how could they, I was being naive again. But, as they left for home, reality caught up with me. If just one had understood part of the evening, it had been worthwhile. I hoped they had.

They could not have understood the emotions. Lambing in February with the utter satisfaction of helping a ewe produce fine lambs that leap to their unsteady feet in seconds reassures my faith in life. It also brings the disasters. The lambs that try to live through difficult births but just don't make it. The ewes that find the whole ordeal too much and the one that doesn't bother. At the end of each day, I collapse into bed, my mind alive with flashing thoughts of great joy and sorrow, intertwined in hideous harmony. My body is crying out for sleep - if only I could.

As with most things, systemisation is important in the lambing yard, not only for efficiency, but also to maintain health standards and keep at bay those bacterial infections that lurk behind every door and can swoop through the whole flock in hours. As I knew the flock was growing well and the fear of a failed sale in October receded in my mind, I remembered what had made it so.

Joe had arrived late one afternoon, unfolding his tall figure from the battered old car. Lambing was reaching its peak, tiredness was growing and finding fault was easier. Robin and Eleanor were returning from the lambing yard, chatting, happy and relaxed. Superstition has more power at lambing time than any other. When things are going well, everyone knows it is only a knife edge away from going badly. And new ideas, new ways and new people threaten this balance. Joe, innocently arriving to take up his new lambing job, was that threat.

Robin and Eleanor greeted him sceptically. Recently asked to leave his public school for being found in the local convent once too often, Joe seemed to have little in common with Robin, the third son of a Galloway hill farmer, or Eleanor, risen from holiday work to top student and viewing the farm as her own.

'He won't do', she said, after only a day, as we took breakfast and Joe rested after taking the night shift. 'I don't think he knows enough.'

'I wouldn't rely on him', added Robin. Robin, who was due to leave within the week to take another lambing post in Scotland, viewed handing over to this limp Dorset lad as sacrificing all his effort. The necessary balance was creaking. By late afternoon we were all on duty, getting clear and preparing for a busy night.

'There is a ewe in trouble over here', called Eleanor. Robin stepped forward till a glance from me stopped him.

'Joe, I think this is yours.'

He worked for nearly an hour, with Eleanor holding the head and throwing doubtful glances to Robin, who leant on the gate as a judge in a courtroom, with the guilty verdict written on his face. Joe was of few words, sometimes he looked lost, often in doubt, but eventually the glow of success showed in his smile.

'Here it is', he said, triumphantly, pulling two feet and a nose gently into view. The rest was easy - two live lambs - but more, much more, was the respect of the gang. Within days, humour reigned in the yard. Confident that we could handle whatever nature threw at us, we enjoyed the most successful lambing I have known.

As Robin left, he shook Joe by the hand. 'Good luck', he said, as one professional to another. I knew the success had not been accidental, but because we had seen the problems before they became problems and laughed as we did so.

March and April brought not only the end of lambing, but the onset of those clear, sunny days when everything bursts out with growth, but also cold north winds and late snow. Our lambs of the hardy Texel breed can cope with any weather, so long as their stomachs are full of milk. Correct feeding of the ewes is vital and, as the lambs grow away and dance with the first rays of sun breaking on a spring morning, I feel not only satisfaction that I got it right, but joy that the ram selection was right too, at least most of the time.

In June, the lambs were weaned from their mothers and grew away on the most nutritious feed I could produce. Drought always threatens and, as Bed and Breakfast guests come down on cloudless mornings and comment smilingly that it will be another scorching day, my fears are never far away. Sales start in late August and go on into October. They involve selling rams individually to other farms at especially organised auctions, to be used either to improve the meat qualities of their cross-bred flock, or to work on their own pedigree animals. Price variation can be considerable. The breeding details, the appearance and the history of the flock all interact to decide whether the ram makes a high price or a low one. There is no subsidy or guarantee; this is the free market at its most free.

The end of June brings the Royal Show. Since we developed our flock of sheep and classes have been available, we have made an annual sojourn to this highly prestigious event. That it is expensive, and we have never won, once made us stand back and reconsider. With a family illness and young children, we did miss a year, but such were the comments from local farmers that we returned. This year, following our successes in May and with the sale rapidly approaching, would be more important than ever. We did not expect to win, but we must put up a good show in what would be the strongest classes of any breed. Our best young ewes and rams had been selected in April and tended with extra care and attention. The old tup was to have his final show outing and was being gently brought forward for the big day. Showing is not just to win prizes, but to show the type of sheep you produce to potential customers.

Few actual sales result, but the build up to autumn sales has begun and a favourable impression sown here can mature into a good sale later. Although the show lasts nearly a week, the actual competitive showing is over in a day. The remainder is taken up by welcoming visitors, offering hospitality to local farmers suffering from sore feet and dry throats and, occasionally, recovering from a good barbeque the night before. Our lambs put on a good show but were smaller and younger than most and we were pleased to be in the top third. The old ram, Shah, had won a County Show in June and we had high hopes.

He had rested in his pen since our arrival on the Saturday morning. A cool breeze during Sunday had suited him well, but already the early haze that had heralded Monday morning had burnt off and the sun was glaring through. Shah has always hated the heat. Since his purchase as a lamb at the Lanark sales, he has been twice the sheep on cool, damp, drizzly days than in the heat - and today was hot! We had woken him early with a good feed, oats and soaked pulp, with a good bundle of freshly cut vetches. His face and legs had been washed and most of the straw removed from his dense wool.

'Breakfast!', Chris called from the back of the lorry two rows away. I stood back and watched him rest, enjoying his breakfast a second time, as he rhythmically chewed his cud, a sign of health and contentment in a sheep.

As the time of his class approached, a clean, white halter was slipped over his head, an operation he never approved of, and he was walked from his pen. Some sheep were uneasy, throwing their heads, looking to graze or run; others took a healthy interest, as a horse before a big race, they knew something was going to happen. Shah seemed more interested in going to sleep, lying his ears lazily against his head, and easing back on his hind legs in a most unflattering way. I wiped his face with some cold water.

'Come on, Shah. Wake up, boy.' He looked at me with resigned superiority.

'I will decide on that'.

There were fifteen in the class, drawn up in a line facing the judge, as he made his way from one to another, checking mouths and feet, feeling width and eyeing the length, taking in the balance of the sheep and comparing it with the others. Initially, Shah was drawn out third, but, as the heat penetrated his initial resolve and the weight of his well-developed hind quarters - the best in the class - showed in his tired legs, he was moved to fifth.

'I liked him', said the judge afterwards, 'and on a cool day he might have risen two places, rather than dropped two.' With this to sustain us, we led the panting old sheep through the growing crowds to his pen.

The Royal is well known for many facets of farming and rural life, and well up among these is the flower show. Late one evening, early in the show, we were drinking and putting the world to rights with friends in the cosy confines of a cattle lorry. Many exhibitors convert their stock transport into living accommodation, and many years' experience has allowed this to combine simplicity with amazing comfort. Chris has become as well known for her visits to out-of-bounds areas as for her night owl tendency. Gretta has a similar character and the conversation edged towards a night-time visit to the flower show. Picturing the acquisition of armfuls of flowers and the resultant discovery of holes in vital displays the next day, this sortie was met with an instant ban. Girls do not appreciate bans, and Chris and Gretta are not ordinary girls. They left ten minutes later, having agreed not to touch anything, and arrived at the gate at two in the morning. The security guard was checking in judges and assumed they were among them.

'What's your name?', running his finger down the list of expected adjudicators.

'There', said Chris, pointing.

'Right', he said, 'do you know where to go?' The girls nodded and walked away confidently. It was not until they took a wrong turn that their true identity was discovered and full feminine charm was needed to persuade their escort to continue the tour.

Their humour and bonhomie lightened a long night for the guide and a friendly atmosphere developed as their tour progressed. The final exhibit at the end of a long marquee was an elaborate design made entirely of sweet peas in many colours. The man had just finished and stood to admire his work. Several buckets of spare blooms were grouped to one side and, as they made to leave, the man offered them one. Pictures of our reaction upon their return with these flowers brought out their wicked best and they readily accepted. Our reaction was predictable and the laughter that followed, infectious. Anyone trying to sleep in neighbouring lorries would have a rude awakening but then, they should have known better than to park there anyway.

At some time during the week I invariably suffer from alcoholic sunstroke. A blend of too many late-night barbecues and too much trying to be polite during the heat of the day. Visiting farmers, customers past, present and hopefully future, rest their legs, sit in a soft chair and drink a can of chilled beer. A welcome break from the dust and concrete of the show. As they sit, regain their breath and the feeling in their feet; as their throats lose their likeness to sandpaper, I wonder if they appreciate the other side of the show. I doubt if they can. They can't know the joy of producing a sheep, seeing it born, grow and gain a prize. Of laughing together, whether show champion owner or totally unmentioned. Of waiting for all the commercial farmers and hangers-on to troop off home with bundles of pamphlets in glossy bags, then sitting back ourselves, a deep intake of breath, and saying, 'Yes, the day can begin'. When all are gone and sheep are safely loaded, we climb aboard, turn the key on the week with hope and shout, 'Till next year'. Perhaps it will be our year.

Our return from the Royal, just a week into July, met with our busiest period for Bed and Breakfast. Visitors from every corner of the globe descended on us in every shape and size. Fishermen came in greater numbers as the warm weather brought the best out of the fish. During these busy times, most faces became merely names in the visitors' book, memory fading under the weight of new guests. Occasionally, memory will stick and concentrate with time.

In the last week of July, three Aussie girls came to stay. In some ways, they fitted the image of the typical Australian group 'doing' Europe. They carried their much-travelled ruck sacks, wanted the cheapest rooms and wore confident smiles that were totally reassuring. Yet they were not school leavers or newly retired, the ages that most populate this colonial run. Nearer to forty than thirty, they carried the confidence of age on young faces.

Ros was several inches taller than her companions and stood a little apart from them. Though not classically beautiful, her eyes were of the softest blue and so deep that when you looked into them, you felt you were actually looking into her. They could absorb and almost hypnotise you, lift you into the clouds and then gently lower you to the ground with a broadening smile.

Chris had taken rams to the first sale of the season and our young dog had gone missing. After arriving in early evening, Ros asked the way around the village to take in the last of the evening light. I found myself accompanying her on the pretext of finding the dog. My search was far from diligent and, as we passed the church and made our way down into the valley, I felt very at peace with the world. Conversation flowed from the depths of mental care, in which she was a nurse, to the heights of angloaussie humour and the future cricket tour. Her hair was naturally wavy and seemed to bounce along with her personality. Her gait was light and springy and carried her broad shoulders with confidence. Her face carried little make up and, when I could force my gaze from those eyes, it showed the signs of departing youth and past strain. It was a face that could have told a story but chose to lock it behind the eyes and smile. There was a lot of hurt in there and I wanted to know.

We crossed the bridge and climbed the narrow path that rises up the southern side of the valley. Near the top, we sat at the seat provided for people to rest during their ascent and looked back across the valley. Lights were already showing the coming of night. How long had we been out? I didn't want to know. Her face was now just an outline but I could feel in her voice that she was relaxing, becoming more open; the facade was going with the day, yet I knew it could shut as a clam at the slightest sign of threat.

I spoke of schools, children, parents. Leading into a conversation and letting her take over and make the pace. Episodes of happiness would herald times of worry that had been bottled up for too long, but I knew these were not the bottom of her pain. She was still testing the water, looking for reassurance that taking the plunge would not add to her suffering. I realised she was holding my hand and now squeezing hard. How long she had held it I don't know, but I could feel a tremble in her grip and felt the flood of tears erupt inside her. We embraced without speaking, the warmth of her tears soaking my shirt and stinging my face. The love for a man killed five years before in a motor accident had finally broken through in a tidal wave of emotion. Words followed in a semi-coherent flood, which I dared not interrupt. It was not meant to be understood or challenged; it was a statement of her undying love for someone who was gone forever.

I passed her my hanky and, as she wiped her tears, I could sense a new smile below those superb eyes. A smile of relief. It was raining by the time we returned to the house and all was asleep and dark. I made us both a hot chocolate, we deserved it. With her half-drunk mug she stood to leave and took my hands. We looked into each other's eyes for only a few moments and yet they spoke more words than any book.

In the morning, it was as if the night had never been. She and her friends poured over maps and itineraries, breakfast was eaten, bills were paid. They loaded their small rental car and started the engine. It was only then that, from a half open window, Ros said thank you. She didn't speak and her smile was not noticeably broad, but last night was here again and I knew would always be so.

Chris returned from her trip to Wales. Old friends had welcomed her, and old customers had returned to bid for our sheep. Yet the trade was depressed and did not bode well for the new season. Posters and hand-outs for our on-farm sale had arrived and were being used at every show and sheep event we attended. Chris had only taken four sheep to the Welsh sale; nearly a hundred remained with the sheep for our own sale on top of that. The lull that had descended on us with the summer showing and influx of guests, was now threatened by approaching storm clouds.

In my dreams, I would check and re-check every aspect of the sheep - their rations, their health, the overall arrangements – and, having thus battened the metaphorical hatches, would drift into a short, deep sleep. An increasing proportion of our sales are agreed privately on the farm, to local farmers or past customers returning for more. These not only save on the costs of transport, time and commission at sales, but allow a more personal bond to develop between buyer and seller. The type of ram best suited to a farmer's system can be discovered over time, any problems sorted quickly and the overall satisfaction of on-farm deals brought to the fore.

John and Phil arrived after lunch. They had bought a ram from us the previous year and wanted another. With all our yearling rams available, other than the few Chris had sold in Wales, I asked a good price. They walked slowly through the flock, pointing out this sheep and then another. They certainly seemed to be going for the best. Eventually they turned to me and pointed to a ram in front of them. It was undoubtedly the smallest ram there. I couldn't believe my eyes nor resist asking the criteria they used to make their selection. I didn't want to sound critical and certainly wanted to hide the amazement that I felt. Yes, the ram they had chosen was only worth a fraction of what I'd asked, and why him?

'Oh, he's the quietest and mother will have to feed him', was their answer. I have learnt never to question a buyer's choice.

However, with the on-farm sale rapidly approaching, it was important to use the organised national sales as a shop window, to keep our name and sheep increasingly evident in front of prospective buyers. As one of the longest-established flocks in the country, we were anxious to extol the breeding qualities of our stock - that many families could be traced back to the first imports of the breed into the country - and to highlight the successful, well-known sires that we had used.

Over the years, we had sold rams and some females to most parts of the country. Having been used to our droughted pastures, these sheep often found their new homes a paradise and our reputation for producing healthy stock that would grow and thrive had developed. The breed was expanding, and many new members were being attracted by the promise the future held. We hoped our reputation would draw some of those anxious to increase their small flocks.

August sales continued the uncertain trade that had been July and, with the main events of early September about to strike, a feeling of resignation hung in the air. The intervening months disappeared into the chaos of farming and guests, with only an occasional flash of anticipation as August drew nearer.

12

CHAPTER TWELVE

Despite having an Australian uncle, we were still new to the ways of Australian life. That strange blend of English fairness and American confidence, which can manifest itself from totally considerate to utterly brash. Mark and Maxine were obviously Quintin's parents, not that either were six-feet-five, but in their lovely blend of lively consideration, carried by a tremendous self-confidence. They arrived in mid-afternoon with Catherine, the daughter in ongoing mourning for the boyfriend left behind, and led by Quintin, who was already showing the bemused and absent look of the bridegroom.

Some friends in the village were away for the week and had agreed to let Mark, Maxine and Catherine use their cottage as a sleeping base. They would take all their meals with us but would have their own freedom. It would also give us the room to put up the best man and his girlfriend in reasonable comfort and allow Quintin to have as much independence from his family as he felt he might need.

Bob Hart arrived later the same afternoon, having just collected Renee from the station. Much shorter and slighter than Quintin, he was a very relaxing young man, from Melbourne not Sydney, who carried that genuine air that made you feel happy and confident in his presence. The sort of man anyone could be happy to have as a best man. Renee was tall, almost as tall as Bob, and, having been born in New Mexico yet worked as an air stewardess, carried that blend of accents that was truly American.

The week before had been punctuated by the problems of food and sleeping arrangements. Chris had drawn up a provisional menu for the week, designed to feed a minimum number at every meal, and went through it sitting opposite me at the breakfast room table.

'I'm not going to do sweets', she said, as if a politician declaring a very daring change in policy. 'I have filled the fruit bowl', pointing to the large porcelain bowl in the corner, overflowing with every kind of fruit imaginable. 'We will have fruit instead.' She turned a page in her notebook, a new chapter.

'Bedrooms', she declared, with as much question in her voice as statement, but she didn't wait for a reply. 'Quintin can have the poppy room.' A room redecorated with poppy-design curtains and quilt, standing out warmly against the plain buttermilk walls. A full-length, gilded mirror picked up the light that flooded through the two high windows and threw reflections onto the shadowed wall. A wonderful room, with a fine, old double bed. A large room even for a large man, but then Hillary might need to come to check on wedding details. I smiled.

'Yes, the poppy room for Quintin', I replied, though I knew no reply was needed.

'Will Renee and Bob be sharing?' This was definitely a question and one to which I had no immediate answer. Does a girl fly all the way from New Mexico to be with a boy who has flown all the way from Melbourne, to sleep alone?

'They are both in their twenties.'

'Yes', I pronounced with exaggerated confidence. 'They can always put a bolster down the middle.'

We were wrong.

Yes, the bolster went down the middle, but the idea that we should assume they wanted to sleep together offended Renee's American innocence. She forgave us, and has been a dear friend ever since, but it has shaken my inner ability to judge human nature.

The wedding came and went with smooth predictability. A marquee on the lawn allowed Hillary's parents to entertain at home and the caterers did well enough but, as the evening approached, I could feel the young natives growing restless. We drove the three miles home knowing that the party invasion would not be far behind. Too many young people had behaved too well, for too long, for the night to pass quietly. Once away from the respectability that had been the day, I knew they had to let go. The cellar had been made ready in its timeless party way, and sleeping bags and quilts hauled out for those who would not be able to go home.

By the morning, most of the floor space in the house was taken up by recumbent bodies; some had even spread into Bob and Renee's room, adding insult to Renee's injury. But, as I look back on the wedding, my memory is not of the day or the night, but of the evening before. Throughout the week, Mark and Maxine had countered any act of kindness by Chris and I with the promise of outstanding hospitality when we next go to Australia. With two young children to bring up and educate, as well as a farm to run, such promises, although sincerely uttered, began to have a hollow ring about them. It was, therefore, with great pleasure that we accepted their invitation to dine with them on the Friday night at the Randolph in Oxford.

Situated on the corner of St. Giles and Beaumont Street, the Randolph has not only been Oxford's most famous hotel to me, but also the place we parked the car when grandmother took me for toasted tea cakes at the old Cadena, or where my father took my mother for an indulgent drink before he courted her to the Ritz. I had never ventured beyond its imposing facade and this choice of venue added greatly to the fantasy, the total unreality of the week.

We were booked for eight and arrived at seven-thirty. I searched the bars, no one. We bought a drink as eight approached and a spotty youth, already too tall for his waiter's trousers, came enquiring for Mark's party. Satisfied that there must be some unavoidable delay, he disappeared, and we had another drink, trying to take in the steady flow of diners that were being served drinks by a young barman with a permanent smile. I could picture him at the dentist, drill whining and still with that precast smile. They finally arrived just before ten, their trip to the Cotswolds culminating in taking the A34 north, instead of South, with the ensuing horror of entering Stratford when they should have been entering Oxford.

We moved promptly to our table, the two old aunts avoiding the window, the rest of us only too grateful to sit down and eat. A wine waiter soon appeared with a smile from the same factory as his cocktail-bar colleague. Mark was a well-known connoisseur of wine and soon ordered for the first course. The order for the second course involved more conversation from the waiter and growing exasperation from Mark. When the waiter returned for the third time, it was apparent that all was not well. Looking back, I can see the Australian language and accent as second only to the Irish for being suitable for swearing without sounding totally offensive.

'I don't spend eighteen thousand dollars a year on wine for a shit like you to tell me what I like, now piss off.'

There was no real anger or malice in Mark's voice, the words had simply been used to call a spade a spade, and used quietly. I was full of admiration, not only for Mark's ability to rise above situations and defuse them in that all-Australian way, but especially for the waiter who, smile still intact, left with a courteous 'Certainly, Sir', as if despatched for another bottle of claret.

~~~~~~~~~~~~~~~~~~~

The end of the long school holiday brought a reduction in visitors. Families en route to holidays in Cornwall or a trip to see granny in Blackpool, dried up. The most rewarding had been the young families from far north, deciding the journey too far to do in one hop and breaking the trip here. Young children are glowing with anticipation, adrenalin already adding to furtive imaginations. Their minds rarely give us more than a fleeting visit before rushing into the future.

I often wonder how well the actual holidays match up to the self-preparation and expectations that take full hold in this house. Sometimes, the same families will stay with us on the return trip too. You can gauge from the children how things have gone. Parents are now tired and concentrating on the practicalities of arriving home and returning to work. Stoic cheeriness rules their faces and, whether things have gone well or have been an unmitigated disaster, their attitudes are similar. The children will also be tired but instances will break out through this tiredness; one child will challenge another's story and suddenly the dam of their shyness will break into the flood waters that were their holiday.

Between the cornflakes and bacon and egg, a week of human success and failure, seen through totally human eyes and with as many dimensions as there are children, will hit you. There is no need to contribute to this dialogue, an occasional nod of the head, grunt or amazed smile will be perfectly adequate. I invariably find this to have a therapeutic effect on me, if not on the parents who are trying to organise their family for the final stage of their journey home. I can leave the house and before I have reached the barn, some hundred yards distant, my brain will have filed the torrent of opinion, laughter, recrimination, disappointment and elation that make any holiday. I will have been there with them. A fly on the wall with access to their thoughts and, as I start the tractor, I too feel rejuvenated and sometimes decidedly tired.

~~~~~~~~~~~~~~~~~~~~

Just as the river stretched upstream of the farmhouse and buildings, forming the boundary as well as the backbone of the farm, so it runs through the village immediately downstream of the house. The farmhouse is undoubtably part of the village and, by definition, so is the farm itself. Many farmers who live in isolated situations envy the civilisation, proximity to shop, school and church, and the chance to be part of a community that they lack. Likewise, many who are farming as part of a community will look warmly towards the freedom of their isolated neighbours. As they say, the grass is always greener!

A hundred years ago, there would have been four farms based in the village; now, we are the only one left. In the days of the horse, when much work was done by hand, the farms would have been the main employer. In a drawer in the Sitting Room, there is a small, insignificant looking notebook with a soft, fading cover. Inside is laid out in exquisite handwriting the method to measure land area using acres, rods, poles and perches; further on, a list of wages paid for any given area. Written in the eighteen-sixties, it was from a time when a man was expected to scythe an acre of grain a day and his wife would tie it into bundles or sheaves. Since then, farms have become much less important as employers, but have still retained part of their social responsibility.

In an ever-changing world, they are seen as something stable, rock-like, often taken for granted, but necessary nonetheless. A few years ago, I could have also written respected but, somehow, farmers have been portrayed as villains in recent times and, as the population that has known the farm and come to understand it have been replaced to some extent by a more transitory and wary breed, who are happier believing the media than their own eyes, the natural bond of duty and trust has been weakened.

My ancestors played an important part in the organisation of the village, on the hall committee, the parish council and, especially, in the church. I will always picture my mother's face when I told her I had been elected a church warden, somehow renewing a vow with the past, putting another tie in the wall. I remember my first service as a warden. I had been delayed with the sheep and arrived a few minutes late. As I slid, semi-breathless into the pew, John Smith, a recently retired landowner from just outside the village, sidled over with a broad grin.

'I'm so pleased to see you are upholding the family tradition, your grandfather and great-grandfather were always late.'

The custodian attitude that must pervade a family farm is also vital if a village is to keep its self-respect. As the world changes and ground rules seem as solid as sand, the importance of maintaining faith with the past becomes increasingly important. I can see the changes we are making at Manor Farm, mirrored by the pressures that are straining the community around us. The common bond of employment is long gone and, increasingly, the understanding of the land-based community has slipped away. There are some who oppose any change on the farm, who want it to stay as it has been, like a museum that can somehow be immune to the forces of the world around. Others see the farm as a nuisance, with unpleasant smells or slow tractors. But, as they rush to their work, it is obvious that these people view the community with the same disdain. They have taken the art of self-motivation to its ultimate conclusion.

We are a friendly village. The shop is a happy place to visit, the church welcoming and well used, a wave is the norm, not the exception. As I take breath, I can see that the important part of the village, those that care, are still here. They may be quiet but, in many ways, they are the unsung heroes of the village. They have grown accustomed to standing back and letting others take the strain. That may be just a convenient habit, but I prefer to think that they are happy to trust the village to those who have known it and shown they care. As the farm fights to take in the fresh air that the future holds and build on the old foundations, so the village must meet the future. The problems of weekenders and commuters, traditional families and lack of work and housing, will not go away. In many ways, the village needs its farm, and vice versa, more now than ever.

During the summer, many families travel to foreign cottages or sunny beaches, leaving a rear guard of retired old men and village stalwarts to hold off the invader. But they are all back for the Flower Show at the beginning of September. Always held on the lawn of Wootton Place, the former rectory, it is an attempt to keep alive the best of the past, while meeting the needs of the present. In recent years, we have generally been able to miss this combination that comes together as nouveau nostalgia. Chris has been away showing sheep at the Moreton show and I have been selling rams at Shrewsbury.

The inevitable had to happen, of course, when the organisers split ranks as they diverted the calendar towards this weekend or that. Two years ago it happened, and I was caught. We have always been called on to do our bit - straw bales for the bowling, table transport and chairs for the band - but our on-the-day involvement had usually been saved by unavoidable business commitments. I have sometimes wondered where and when I developed this allergy to what should be a joyous village celebration for me. I think it stems, as do many allergies, from a boyhood experience.

My grandfather would wander for hours up the rows of mangels. Ostensibly grown for winter sheep feed, I soon became convinced that these ancient beet were really here to cause summer holiday torture. He would stop occasionally, measure the root with his stick, and then either leave a marker or wander on. In due course, a day or two before the show, I would be sent to pull these huge earthbound plants, carry them to the yard and wash them. He would then come as a Sergeant Major, looking critically along the line of gleaming roots with leaves as hair, tied carefully with baler twine, with big bows. If they had been marked or a leaf broken during these preparations, the stick would tap the offending part as if goading it into recovery and then he would look at me with that 'Now look here, boy' glance. He would finally select his best three and I would load them into the ancient stable cart and pull them through the village, over the deep gravel in front of the old house and onto the well-manicured lawn. The smell of newly mown grass and wet canvas would be compromised by glorious scents drifting from ancient shrubberies.

The show marquee was always on the furthest part of the huge lawn, a lawn once used as the cricket field and where my grandfather hit a six into a passing baker's dray and had to run after it. A story which grew with the telling, as my arms ached with the pulling across this soft surface. The mangels were laid out in front of the marquee, where a small notice read: 'Three mangels, to have been grown within the parish'. We were always last or last but one. We grew a modern variety, which was smaller but higher in sugar and, as the judges who were probably doubling up to judge embroidery and plum jam always went by size, the result was inevitable.

My grandfather would rant about quality before reminding me to collect the wretched things the next morning. I would cut them up and throw them into the chickens, who pecked at them with the same relish we would eat a melon on a hot day. At last, I would think, some pleasure from those old roots. We no longer grow mangels.

At the end of the afternoon, with the judging completed and prizes awarded, most of the entries were retrieved by their exhibitors; those that were left were auctioned. When, as a boy, I played farms with my brother and friends, we would always have to start with a sale of stock and machinery and I would be auctioneer – a job for which I have carried a subconscious desire ever since. I was, therefore, quite happy to act as stand-in auctioneer for the year. The goods often lacked natural excitement; a bunch of French beans, six huge onions or a jam tart with the judge's slice neatly missing. I looked for the star around which to build this prestigious sale and found it in a huge fuchsia. Standing some four feet high, it was a truly glorious plant, cascading with big, colourful blooms.

A lady came up to me.

'How much will it make?' I looked reproachful.

'I know several are interested in it', I whispered, though no one was remotely in earshot.

'Should I get my cheque book?', she replied.

I nodded. Now to find another bidder and I looked around. My father was examining it and I felt wicked. I tried to hurry through the preliminary lots, putting several together when initial interest was poor. Several bid for the fuchsia but soon only my father and the lady remained. Both were bidding with great subtlety, it could have been Christie's, and when I finally knocked it down to my father for twenty-two pounds, he felt sure I had run him. Whenever I walk through his garden, he will point out another fuchsia, a cutting from this famous plant, as if saying, 'that makes it only two pounds a plant now', justifying his outlay.

Good land will have poor buildings and poor land, good buildings, according to the old saying. This, I understood to mean you could let a good farm, despite poor buildings, but to let a poor farm, good buildings would be needed to find a tenant. Certainly, Manor Farm had been equipped with a wealth of buildings. A wide access yard leads away from the farmhouse. To its right sit the old buildings, dating from between the seventeenth and early nineteenth centuries. To the left, a model set of buildings crafted in hand-cut stone had been added in the mid nineteenth century. Ten years ago, the first testing of the ground between the farm and the village was exposed when we applied to convert the latter set of buildings to houses. Ours is a far from unique experience. The problems of aging, inappropriate buildings, the restrictions of a conservation area, the need of a farm to reinvest and the natural opposition by villagers to change, all supplied the ingredients for a fractious situation. The buildings, which were south facing and, as an estate agent would say, 'occupying a prime position', were well beyond their best. Described in the sale brochure of the nineteen-twenties as being in 'immaculate condition', the roofs were now going as the batten nails rusted and the walls were bowing in places, a sorry sight.

Yet, through this surface aging, the natural balance still showed. Curved, cut-stone windows; arched bays and fine, old wood that were features of their time. A time now replaced by raw steel in totally functional, umbrella-like hangars. Farming could not afford the nostalgia to keep these in good order, but they should not be lost. Conservation was the only answer. I wasn't sure. The architect produced drawings of how they could once again be proud, useful, cared for.

My father had given a lifetime to these buildings; seen memories come and go, the good times and the bad. Was I asking him to amputate part of himself, to let strangers into the farm cordon that has existed for so long? Was it a retreat, the first sign of betrayal, of the end? Or was it something else? The end, perhaps, of the 'my farm is my kingdom' era and the acknowledgement that business had crept almost unnoticed into the way of life called farming.

'But we still keep cattle in that shed, and where will you put the grain we have always put in this barn?', he would demand, when I broached the subject. He was right, of course, we had always done these things, but now the cost of repairing the old roof was greater than the profit from the cattle and would a new store not keep the grain better? Slowly, I went through the figures, directing him away from the comfort of nostalgia, history and the things we had known, towards what the future might hold - efficiency, economics, simplicity - just as I had directed and convinced myself only days before. We walked through the barn and I noticed him stop.

'I know all this means a lot to you', I said, turning.

'No', he replied, tapping the stone wall. 'This means nothing, it's what it stands for that matters. If you and your brother can achieve what you want from life by selling this, then let it go. I have had my time.'

We walked on. I could see he was still uncertain, he hadn't finished.

'But before you throw away the past, make sure you like the future, there will be no second chance.' A Scotsman through and through, I had never thought of my father as a philosopher, now I saw him in a new light.

I knew my father wanted to retire. I had a young family, as did my brother. The time for choosing had come and must be grasped. I knew it and didn't want to. I showed the professional plans to my father, the barns as houses, with people and trees, and to these I added the dimension of potential sale value and what it could achieve. His scepticism fuelled my determination. His natural reluctance to change mellowed as he saw the possibilities and then turned to doubt. The neighbours wouldn't like it, nor would the planners! I persevered and knew I was winning this battle, the first of many. I called the planning officer in for a personal opinion and, to my surprise, he liked the scheme. He was not the vampire so often described, determined to find fault and say no. His ideas were positive, he shared my admiration for these old constructions and their need for attention.

When the plans, submitted to the district council, were returned for scrutiny by the parish council and village, admiration was not the word on the tip of my tongue. It was not the opposition that I found so depressing, but the reasons for it. No one noticed the buildings, and few even bothered to check the plans to see what we were doing for the future. It was all about cars and parking, access and roads, and general opposition to change. It threatened to become personal.

Late one evening I received a phone call from the chief planning officer. It must be important, I thought, for him to ring so late.

'We've received a letter from the police demanding we refuse you permission for your proposal', he said. I could tell he was annoyed, planning officers don't like being told their job by anyone. And I knew who it was, smiling to myself as I did so. A high-ranking police officer lived just down the road and had already told me his views on our proposals.

'Would you like a copy of the letter? I think you could take the matter further', the planning officer continued. I thanked him but declined. From that moment I was sure planning would be granted and that was all I wanted.

I was confident that, with a cool head, it would come right in the end and the plans were finally passed by the District Council. The barns were converted and, as time passed, the opponents to the scheme began to appreciate the change; the character that showed through, the improved entrance to the village, the view.

One day an old lady came up to me as I stood in the access road to these new houses, looking across the valley. She appeared a little nervous. We entered into general conversation before coming around to the real point she wanted to make.

'I opposed the scheme, but I like it now. I want you to know that.' She almost smiled as she turned and walked away.

The first hurdle of bringing the farm into the present day had been achieved. I had learnt a lot and especially who my real friends were. There was a long way to go and I knew that my duty to the farm, to my family, to the village and to the past would have to be balanced and brought together with my duty to the future. I felt so small, as I still do, so insignificant, and yet I also knew that I was getting there.

CHAPTER THIRTEEN

Early October will always be remembered as the time of the Irish. No ancient customs or tribal rituals, but sheer farce, as can only develop with the Celtic ingredient. The three-day horse event in Blenheim had grown from its embryonic, novice status and was now proclaimed a fully-fledged member of the senior circuit. Our close proximity and yard of stables made us obvious candidates for off-course accommodation. Our name had been sent out with other details and enquiries soon came in.

The Red House, an old brick cottage owned by my parents and tucked in behind the farmhouse garden, had been let out to an American serviceman from the local base. He had recently returned home after his tour of duty and the building was undergoing a facelift before new tenants moved in. Chris soon realised that it would be empty for the horse event and arranged to 'borrow' its two bedrooms to increase our capacity. I had recently taken part in one of the scripted 'Murder Supper Parties' that had been doing the rounds, culminating in full murder weekends at obscure seaside hotels in the depths of winter. As the time of the

Blenheim three-day event drew near, our list of bookings took on the appearance of one of those scripts and a feeling of impending madness hung heavily in the air.

A week before the event, Chris was sitting at the Breakfast Room table, seemingly playing battleships with herself. She called me over, her voice tinged with elation.

'I think I've got it.' I quipped about hoping it was not too painful before realising this was a comment of serious intent and drew up a chair beside her. She explained the logistics of fitting in our cosmopolitan party.

'The Frenchman and his wife can have the Red House. They have a young baby and that will keep it out of screaming range from the rest of us, as well as giving them more privacy.' She was trying to sound benevolent and not succeeding.

'The New Zealand competitor and her mother can have the Blue Room.' A room once blue, but now a floral design with very little blue in it, certain to add to the chaos of the week.

'The Irish lady and her son can have the Poppy Room.' These last guests were expected on the Saturday, but the rest were due at various times over the weekend and early part of the week. Chris was trying to see any gaps, overlaps and chances to fit in one-night visitors.

With the growing pressures of the forthcoming sale and the hectic week ahead, we took the chance to get away on the Saturday and watch the children play for their schools. Chris left in the morning to watch Vicki play hockey and I followed in the afternoon to watch James play rugby. There are few more relaxing or satisfying times than standing on the touch line beside other parents, sharing pride, elation and that essential piece of parental advice that is so easy to give from the comfort of a warm coat and lungs full of air. The ball came loose, a player picked it up but was caught, more players, more bodies.

'Come on, boys!', a disappointed parent shouted, as a penalty was awarded, and the bodies regained their vertical posture.

'You, sir', said the referee, tapping James on the shoulder.

'Me, sir?', replied James, with a hint of mock surprise, as his teammates dragged him back before any signs of dissent could show through.

There is a camaraderie on the rugby field which is found in no other sport. The natural team spirit is somehow enhanced by the close physical contact and the fact that the scrum is an entity that depends on eight individuals. As we returned, I felt a deep sense of inner warmth. It was not just the pleasure of being in from the cold or having enjoyed a second cream cake after the match, but more like a mountaineer viewing the peak through a halo of cloud, a sense of it all being worthwhile.

We had warned Cyril and Dibs, a wonderful couple whose cottage overlooks the farmhouse drive, that the Irish couple might arrive, but were totally unprepared for the five strange cars that stood out as a blanket of contrasting colours from the light in front of the house.

A large grey Mercedes that became more yellow in the light of day, a small black polo, a dirty red Land Rover...

'What have we here?', proclaimed Chris with total calmness. My mind was halfway between the touch line and the sheep, which were awaiting my attention.

'A form of chaos, a bevy of beauties, a tea party?', I added flippantly. How little I knew.

The Breakfast Room was full of strange people enjoying tea, with Kay assuring them that all would be well. Kay is a teacher, a friend and a girl who keeps her horse in the stables. Immediately, the girls set to organising the accommodation and I took on the post of porter, escorting groups to their respective rooms. As the New Zealanders were not expected until Monday, the Blue Room was allocated to a couple returning to London and I led the way up the old staircase. I was confronted by a beautiful young girl coming out of the shower, who smiled, wished me well with a broad Irish accent and carried on down the stairs.

On returning to the Breakfast Room I asked Chris who she was, but was met by a blank look. Then, 'Oh yes, we are expecting the Irish lady and her nineteen-year-old son.'

I was not impressed. Although getting older, I knew the girl whose smile still glowed in the front of my mind was too young to have a nineteen-year-old son. If there is something intriguing in a mysterious girl coming out of the shower in your house, it is certainly enhanced by the Irish accent. The mystery remained until late in the day, when the Irish lady, the expected Irish lady, returned from Blenheim.

'Oh, that will have been Lesley, I told her to come over for a shower. The ones in the shower block are awful.' Lesley was a groom and, as I turned a page of my memory and saw her face, I looked forward to meeting her again.

I left early on the Sunday morning for the last ram sale of the season. I knew Chris would be busy, but I also knew that she was entertaining some amazing people and would be in good hands. The Old Lorry was happier when I left the local lanes with their steep gradients and joined the main road westward. As I travelled at a steady forty miles an hour, with the diesel engine purring hypnotically, my thoughts slowly settled from the frantic heights of the last few days.

With the on-farm sale only three weeks away, the pressure was beginning to tell. I did not feel any conscious worry, I liked to think of myself as a fatalist, but, in the deeper waters of my brain, I knew something was stirring the mud. Occasionally, when I looked into my conscious, the usually clean waters would be cloudy. Sometimes I had that deep, heavy feeling that was almost a headache. I brought myself back to the present as the truck hit a pothole and then concentrated my attention on immediate details. Had I all the paperwork, the passes and the ministry forms? I was going to Builth Wells, to the largest one-day ram sale in the world.

The site of the Royal Welsh show is turned into a sea of tents and parked lorries. Total chaos is always just around the corner and only rigid enforcement of the rules keeps it at bay. The sheep are penned according to their breed and, eventually, I found my allotted pen halfway down an eternally long marquee. It is a tremendous relief to have settled and fed your sheep, parked the lorry and found some friends with whom to share a night cap and sort out the problems of the world. I slept on the top deck of the lorry on an old mattress and in a very snug sleeping bag.

In the morning, as the sun made its watery way over the Welsh mountains, I felt ready for the day. With so many rams on offer and with their natural inclinations not to be the first to make a mistake, the Welsh sheep farmers do not arrive early. Despite the thirty or so breeders who were also feeding their sheep, the marquee seemed empty. My entry of eight Shearling rams was a mixed lot. Four of them were of fair quality, two were rather better, one was worse, and one looked so small that I could not understand why I had entered it at all. The trade at this sale is always fickle and much influenced by the time when your sheep are in the ring. Mine seemed favourably timed so I could only wait, explain their virtues to any would-be buyers and hope.

The trade started predictably slowly but gathered pace after a few good-quality sheep and was levelling well for the season as my time approached. Whilst waiting, I had a good opportunity to study my sheep in more detail than usual. One of the best two increasingly took my eye. I knew he was a son of one of my best ewes and fathered by the old ram we had shown at the Royal. His legs were strong and straight, his muscling well developed, his face powerfully masculine with fine, white hair. In many ways, he was straight from the breeder's manual.

The other sheep that stood above the rest was long and tall, but he lacked the breed points of his colleague. His face was long, his nose narrow and lacked power. Our first sheep in the ring was neither of these and was meant as a pace setter. My favourite followed and the interest showed in the pens was transmitted into bids. At four hundred Guineas, he was knocked down to a small Welshman in the back row. The tall ram followed, strutting around the ring like a stag patrolling his territory. He seemed to stick at three hundred and ninety Guineas but then spluttered on, to four hundred and fifteen. I know the buyer is always right, but it hurt to see a sheep that lacked quality making more money. I dreaded the arrival of my last sheep. He wasn't small, he was minute, and rushed around the ring with ears pricked.

The marquee was now packed with potential buyers, to such an extent that the clerk whose job it was to record prices and buyers had to stand in the ring with the sheep. He was carefully booking the prices and didn't see the sheep approach with head down. It was a superb example of up-ending, as the notes took to the air, before descending like confetti. The man regained his feet, brushing off the straw and ignoring the cheers of the animated crowd.

'A good active sheep, gentlemen, just right for the hill!', shouted the auctioneer.

At two hundred and fifty Guineas it was undoubtedly my most expensive sheep but, as the auctioneer said, the Welsh love an active animal.

I returned with my sheep to the pen. They looked much the same, only a few minutes had passed since the stewards had ushered us out towards the ring, yet now they were part of someone else's plans. At most sales, the fall of the hammer is the end of the day. If any sheep have not been sold, they can be loaded up and taken home. The rest are now the buyer's responsibility. Whether at a good price or not, the seller is free to leave and await his cheque arriving in the post. At Builth Wells it is different. The sheep remain the property of the seller until the buyer comes to collect them and produces his slip, with lot number attached. He is given this when he pays for his sheep and the purpose of this process is to reduce theft. It usually achieves this, but it also achieves an annoying wait for a seller who may have left home the previous morning and have a long return journey to come. I sat on top of the hurdle that made the outside of my pen and felt it digging into my backside. On each side were vendors taking tickets from payers, helping them out with sheep, congratulating them on their purchases and trying to avoid paying luck money. The tradition went on and I sat.

'Would you like a coffee?', said Pam, waving a plastic cup and breaking my melancholy.

'You take sugar, don't you?' Although occupying a pen immediately opposite me, her sheep would not enter the ring for another three hours. The trade would probably have gone and she would struggle to find buyers, yet she retained a bright stoicism that made me feel guilty.

I walked over to her. 'Bill not here?'

'No, he had to go and milk, he'll be back later to load the sheep.' A small man with a cap at an uncomfortable angle stood by my pen and checked its numbers. He was developing a sceptical look, ready to be disappointed. Many are not happy unless they are disappointed, they will have nothing to moan about when they get home. I joined him.

'Can I help you, Sir?'

'Yes, lot 1134', he said, looking down, then surveying the sheep. I knew lot 1134 to be the small one. I smiled to myself.

'So, you were the man who bought him. A good active sheep, I think you'll agree.'

'Ah...yes', was all he said.

I caught the sheep and steered him away from the rest, before the difference in size became more obvious than necessary. The man was not impressed. He spoke to his colleague, as tall as he himself was short, but wearing the same cap.

'A bulk purchase, no doubt', I thought, as they collected the ram, moaned at the pound luck money I gave them and were gone. I wondered if anyone had had a greater day and doubted it.

As the lorry found its way the last five miles home, I felt a happy tiredness coming on. The sheep had all been sold and for a good average. My thoughts turned to Chris and her houseful of guests. I was still trying to imagine the week to come, of all the breeders who had said they would see me at the sale, and I wondered how many would actually make an appearance. The sound of the lorry tyres on the gravel drive brought me back to reality. I suddenly realised how tired I was.

By Tuesday, all of our guests had arrived, and we knew that we had inherited far more than we expected. An ongoing stream of bubbly grooms would descend at the close of day for a shower or bath and, as the chosen restaurant was just across the way, other competitors used us as a base. I discovered that it had been deemed unacceptable for Chris to eat alone on Sunday and she had been taken out with the gang. Monday followed the same routine. Wednesday was the first competition day, yet the approaching event did not dampen the Irish joy of living and their ability to totally relax became infectious. We had invited them to join us for supper that night and they had agreed, on the condition that they bring the drink. It came out of Sarah's car boot by the case and flowed freely.

The first stage, the dressage, went well for most of our guests and especially the Irish. Their spirit hardly needed a boost, but the tempo of life had changed up a gear for the cross country on Saturday. The weather became foul, turning the old Parkland into a quagmire. Vehicles churned deep tracts, as horses struggled to keep their footing. We discovered that the Irish team had taken the lead in the team event with only the show jumping section on Sunday to come. We prepared ourselves for a heavy night. Weary, muddy bodies would pass through the hall en route to any available bath or shower, to be transformed into sparkling and invigorated celebrants, anxious to start the evening of gay abandon. Whether they won tomorrow or not, they intended to make the most of tonight.

Everyone was up early; we to attend to the sheep and the competitors to take their mounts through the veterinary inspection. Some had an early breakfast, some came back for it later, and some managed to consume both. A dry night had improved conditions as jumping got underway. Old, experienced horses had a great advantage over the young, novice rides. Mark, the 19-year-old son had a young and very promising horse but looked upon show jumping as his bogey event. He had several fences in hand, but would they be enough? They still had a lead, with team captain, Kenny, and Mark to go. Mark used up some of the points, but Kenny had a good enough round to ensure the lead was retained. The local band played the Irish national anthem as the team circled their lap of honour. Flowers, medals and champagne were balanced precariously on bouncing saddles.

We were home when the triumphant crew returned. Kenny burst in, champagne in one hand, flowers in the other. 'Chrissy, Chrissy', he shouted, as he ran searchingly around the house. James had been home for the weekend and we took an early family supper before Chris drove him back to school. I was in the kitchen when Kenny entered.

'Come on, Bob, we're off to supper.'

'No, I've already eaten, I'll join you for drinks after.'

They left and I tried to concentrate on some work that I had been putting off. I joined them an hour later, to find they were still only ordering their food and were definitely in need of it. Peter, the landlord, knew them well by now and moved methodically along the table taking their orders, appreciating the jokes he'd heard before. He got to me and I declined his offer to eat.

'I've eaten', I said. Peter smiled, looked up from his pad and glanced along the table, heaving with humour and empty bottles.

'Would it not be an idea to eat again?'

I nodded, realising that food was likely to be my only salvation in this company of such experienced celebrants.

I was sitting next to Lesley, the girl from the shower and, as alcohol clouded our senses, our conversation became deeper and philosophical.

She was looking for her Sugar Daddy, very rich and very old. I knew that beneath all this bravado was a great sense of caring. It extended along the whole table like a breath of fresh, if alcoholic air.

~~~~~~~~~~~~~~~~~~~

Chris left in the morning to drive down into Gloucestershire. Her father's sudden ill health, operation and death had come so quickly. He had seemed so well, only in his early sixties and with so much to live for. Chris had taken it well, but I knew the shock must still be there somewhere, waiting to pounce. Her siblings were all to meet at their father's old cottage, to sort out the loose ends, allocate furniture and come to terms with the finality. I have only a brother and, in many ways, I have envied Chris being one of six. Today I didn't. Throughout the day my mind would flash to their meeting. I could recount the times of friction and disagreement, would they re-emerge?

Chris returned late, enough time for many disagreements, but her face was happy and relaxed. There had been no ill feeling and, as we unloaded a few of her favourite odds and ends from the car, I was relieved. She was coming to terms with her loss and it showed in the practicality that took over the conversation.

Gradually, a list of who was having what took shape. Over the years, individuals had shown a preference for certain items and these had been honoured.

'We are having the dining room table', said Chris. 'We are the only ones with a room to take it', she added, with a laugh that almost turned into tears.

'Oh, and we are having the bees.'

Over the years, Chris's mother had added beekeeping to her long list of interests and, on her death two years before, Chris's father had carried them on. As someone who is terrified of entering a chicken run, I was at a loss to see how Chris would cope with a swarm of angry bees, but decided this was not a time to question the wisdom of this acquisition and smiled supportively.

We travelled down one evening, our light trailer bouncing energetically behind the car. Chris's brother David was meeting us at the cottage with a trailer of his own and, between us, we were to convey the bees to their new home in our valley. I knew nothing of bees and my interest had been limited to a distant respect.

'Why the evening?', I had asked naively.

'Because that's when they are all in the hive, there wouldn't be much point moving the hive with bees out at work. Anyway, they tend not to get so angry at night; we can seal them in, move them, and they should remain quite happy.'

I took this assurance from a knowledgeable helper with hope, rather than confidence. Certainly, the hives were giving off a subdued buzz and, seal in place, having a solid-looking hive between me and them was most reassuring. The hives had been kept at various sites around the village and, as they were collected, stacked on the trailer and roped into position, I began to feel more in charge of the situation.

The road home seemed even more bouncy on our return journey. Every movement, every pothole, sent pictures of hives falling apart, angry bees looking for the transgressor, for me. It seemed almost inevitable that our arrival home would show that one seal had come adrift and an angry swarm was clinging to the side of the trailer. We all stood transfixed. The gentle buzz, previously deadened by the safety of the hive, now seemed so close and threatening. We rang a local beekeeper for advice. He seemed unworried and unimpressed.

'They should be quiet enough now, just shovel them up and put them back in the hive.' I offered to fetch the shovel; no one offered to use it.

Necessity can lead to a form of confidence and, as I moved the bees with an attitude based as much on fatality as hope, I gradually felt better.

By the end, I was almost blazé. The next morning, they sounded happier and within a few days they seemed settled.

Two hives were placed at the corner of the paddock below the house, the others were erected below the lake. On a cool day, they would be silent and I would be tempted to raise their roof, to check they were still in residence. On a warm day, I wouldn't venture within twenty yards, but stood and wondered as the coming and going showed as a shimming haze, a hive of eager industry. It couldn't always be so beautiful, so awesome. We learnt of a swarm that had been found and were available. We phoned and offered a home, it had all been so simple and the empty hive looked so sad and lonely, such a waste. They came in a cardboard box, Bill nonchalantly drawing up in his old ford.

'Just put them by the entrance and they will race in.' He was right, once the small cluster surrounding the queen had ushered her in, the rest followed at great speed. After a cup of tea, he left and Chris rubbed her hands, exuding confidence. I waited for disaster to strike. I only had to wait till morning.

The bees had rejected their hive and taken up residence in a thorn bush, just thirty yards from the hive, but ten yards above the ground.

'Hold the box', said Chris, having retrieved the box they had come in from the coal shed, with the logic that if it was right for the expert, it must be right now. She reached as far as she could with a long stick and started to prod the swarm.

'No, hold it under the swarm and catch it when it falls.' Chris, fully clad in anti-bee gear and with a sufficiently long stick to stand a yard or two away from the likely landing area, definitely had the best of the deal. As I stood, unprotected, with a swarm of bees growing angrier with every prod dancing above my head, I felt a desire to run.

'Don't worry, they don't sting when they're swarming', were the words uttered by Chris, but that seemed so remote, so unlikely, so totally unbelievable that I wanted to laugh.

'I told you they wouldn't sting', she said, as the last bees were returned to their proper hive, and gave me the sort of look a mother gives a child after his first night with the light off. The next day, the swarm was in a neighbour's garden hedge. Chris retrieved them easily, she was becoming quite an expert now. But why did they keep moving, what was wrong with our hive? Another neighbour phoned the next morning.

'There's a swarm of bees in my garden, will you remove them?'

He was quite the most grumpy man, newly moved in and, we hoped, soon to move out again. There were no thanks, no request, just an instruction to remove them. His round, chubby face did not suit his arrogant manner, his ongoing anger with life.

The bees were at the top of a young fir tree, almost inaccessible, and very angry in the growing breeze. It was as if the man's anger was permeating the whole garden.

'Well, they've got to be removed. Whose are they, where have they come from?' The effort of retrieval, the man, the bees, the experience, had become enough.

'I haven't the faintest idea,' said Chris, as she left. 'Perhaps you could contact the council.'

By the next day, the bees had moved on. I hoped they found contentment somewhere.

After a time, Chris asked the advice of an expert. He came, went round the hives with her, showed her how to take the honey and how to separate it from the comb. We hired a small separator and, as I turned the handle and the first honey glistened into the bucket below, a definite feeling of success hung in the air. We had our own labels printed to go on the jars and they certainly went down well at the breakfast table.

Very soon we became at home with the bees, though our ignorance was hovering below the surface and one day had to raise its head.

I went out to work early on a summer's morning. A bright, ambitious day, when everything seemed possible. Chris was laying the table ready for the guests, when she realised she was out of honey. She knew the hive nearest the house was ready to have its honey removed and, in a moment of reckless over-confidence, decided to attend to it before breakfast.

Removing honey from a hive is a simple operation for an expert and relatively easy for a novice, providing some basic precautions are taken. They include wearing the correct face mask and gloves, light shiny trousers on which bees cannot get a grip, and no perfumes or creams that might attract the bees. In her enthusiasm, Chris failed to make sure her mask was bee-proof; forgot that her dark, corduroy trousers were ideal runways and climbing ladders for bees, and was unaware that the Morning Primrose she had applied to her face liberally that morning would have the effect it did.

The screams that reverberated along the yard had to be associated with a gruesome murder. I found her clawing at her face shield, which had more bees inside it than out, and with columns of bees marching meaningfully up her trousers. Much brushing and water cleared the offenders, to leave several stings as evidence and a deeper respect for these unique creatures. They and the honey have become part of our life, if a small part. They certainly fit well in our order of things.

14

CHAPTER FOURTEEN

Every farmhouse had an attic - that area between the first floor and the roof deemed suitable only for storage. Into it, every item that was not immediately wanted but which was too good to throw away, was carefully stacked, ready for eternity. I can still remember my grandmother organising its annual spring clean. This was no mere store, no dump of unwanted items, but a carefully maintained appendage to the house below. But, as the plaster between the roof battens began to fall away, and the pace of life made such things as spring cleaning the attic impossible, the store took on a far sorrier appearance under our watch.

It was a Sunday morning after church, and I was a boy again. The sun was shining softly after early showers and Michael Parsons had come for his weekly constitutional. A local farmer and much-loved character, he drank 'Gloucesters' - a blend of gin and cream sherry in equal proportions - in a large tumbler, and happily left the problems of the present to dip into his enlightened past. A great teller of country anecdotes, an expert on first world war battleships and a philosopher on how mankind had lost its way. He was also a great authority on farming, with regard to sporting matters, and a proponent of using corrugated asbestos for all roofs. Amongst this deep and sincere experience, he knew about Stonesfield slate roofs. Ours was such, and he looked at me with a grin.

'A Stonesfield roof lasts ninety years', he said. 'It's the oak pins that hold the battens that go. The damp air soaks the plaster that rots them. When the battens slip, the roof is gone.' I knew he was not just making casual conversation.

'It lasts three generations: the first puts it up, the second enjoys it and the third repairs it. It's just your luck to be the first in the cycle. Yes, you need a new roof', and he held out his glass for a refill.

As a listed house, we needed permission for any changes to the roof. The roofers suggested replacing the old slates, which were very scarce and expensive, with a new reconstituted type. As a three-storey building, the difference would be barely noticeable from the ground and it was certainly the only way we could afford it, so we approached the authorities with this proposal. I can remember Chris clearly, waiting for the right official to be found and then quietly putting our case. I soon realised from her face that all was not well.

'It must be done totally in old slate', the man stated, in a low, expressionless voice.

'But we can't, there are not enough slates and we couldn't afford them anyway', Chris replied, still calm, but determined. The man thought for a moment and then spoke again.

'I have the answer. We will do it for you and send you the bill.'

He went silent, as though he had said enough, sorted a major problem. Chris was too amazed to reply. She sat, dumbfounded, checking what he had said lest she had misunderstood.

'You are not serious? How will that help? We will still have to pay and we can't afford it', she said finally, emphasising the last few words as one might to a child who has not listened.

He was annoyed that we had not welcomed his miraculous solution and took on the air of the man who must be obeyed.

'Well, if you can't afford it, you had better sell it to someone who can!', he stated, with a voice even lower and more expressionless.

Steam started to seep from Chris's ears. She turned the colour of the red roses in the vase behind her as she took breath, and I turned away, as one might before an impending explosion. Chris had my full support and yet my humanity could only feel for this little man. He could not have known nor have been prepared for the wave of emotion and conviction that raged down the line. He tried to sidestep by saying that communities were about buildings and not people, but this only fuelled the tirade. I could hear the Chris I had first known. Once again on the debating podium, slowly softening with well-chosen words and sound reason and then, with impeccable timing, driving home her argument with total power and conviction. I could sense token resistance.

I almost admired him for that but knew the outcome would have to be retreat. He finally suggested putting old slate on the front and new on the back of the house. As the back is four times the area of the front, we accepted, and duly received written confirmation of this. The cost was more than we had hoped but, with the grant, became acceptable.

The attic needed clearing but, as always, I had left it to the last minute. For days, the knowledge that I should get on with the job had been shelved, in favour of those jobs that couldn't wait. Now the attic itself was an emergency, with less than a week before the roof was to be removed, and I stood on the landing at the top of the old oak staircase. To my left was the big attic, a space with half the floor area of the house and with the water tanks hissing disharmoniously in the centre. Chinks of light threw crazy lines on the dusty heaps but seemed irrelevant in contrast to the flood of sun, which was now bathing the room through its one window.

I looked about me. Where should I start? What system? I fought my way to the window. It opened with surprising ease and, for a moment, I stood gazing across the valley towards the tall trees of Blenheim. This was no time for distraction, there would be plenty enough of those before the day was through. I turned myself to the job in hand and smiled at Eleanor, who had arrived as chief assistant.

'Any obvious rubbish can be thrown out of the window and onto the lawn', I declared, as I leant out of the window to check we wouldn't be decapitating the roses in the process. 'Good stuff will be loaded onto the trailer and taken to a stable.'

'What about the in-between stuff?', said Eleanor, looking about her and coming to the obvious conclusion that most of the attic contents would come into this category. I thought of putting it to one side and asking Chris's opinion, but knew that as soon as we entered a discussion, we would be here for ever.

'There will be no in-between stuff', I said, with as much confidence as I could muster. 'This is a time for decisions.'

I smiled at Eleanor, who looked unconvinced at my rhetoric. On the top of most heaps were the most recent additions. Carrier bags of clothes grown out of by the children and put away for a jumble sale. Boxes of odds and ends, drawer contents emptied in a hurry as a piece of furniture had been needed elsewhere. Ninety percent rubbish, but occasionally something of real value. Eleanor thought I was slow and insufficiently ruthless. She carried the impetuosity of youth, the underlying confidence that today was all-important and tomorrow to be valued, but that yesterday was gone and should be forgotten. I tried not to look all-knowing, but I had seen too many yesterdays to be willing to throw them all away without a care. A box of old newspapers caught Eleanor's eye and she moved to lift it with the joy that this, at least, was something she could safely throw out of the window.

'Wait', I called, and lifted a newspaper from the top of the pile.

'Rommel driven back in North Africa', the headlines stated. We had to look again.

If in doubt, an item would come into the 'good stuff' category. This entailed carrying it down two flights of stairs, as opposed to a simple lob out of the window and the satisfying crash that followed. As the morning grew into afternoon, so the heap of rubbish grew on the lawn outside and the sunlight became a wall of floating ancient dust. We were getting down to the older items, long-left chests and boxes, maps in long tubes and parts of tables. My grandmother had been an ardent sale attender, ever on the lookout for that bargain or article she had always wanted. The fact that it would probably be lotted with several articles that no one wanted was of no significance. They could always be put in the attic!

Of far greater interest were boxes that had belonged to individual ancestors. My great-grandfather had lived in the village of Steeple Aston for many years. The boxes of old records, church magazines and everyday correspondence were a character in microcosm. I could easily have sat on a chest and spent the day idly going through them. But today was for action, so, with a mark in my mental calendar to do just that in the near future, they were loaded up and put into store. I decided we needed goals to aim at, or we would be drowned in this sea of nostalgia.

'We will get to this corner today', I proclaimed, as Eleanor returned from another trip down the mountain.

A heap of old paintings and empty frames blocked our way. As I touched them, the sound of broken glass falling between them and onto the floor triggered the 'handle with care' in my mind. An empty trunk stood nearby and they were carefully moved into it. We could hardly see where we had been. Only a small corner of this ever-larger room had been cleared and the lawn below would have been a disgrace to Steptoe.

The next day, we made more progress as the system fell into gear, or was I really becoming more ruthless? I knew that we were having to work to a timescale rather than a standard and that much of what was going into store would itself be rubbish. Yet the fear of throwing away an important document or priceless family heirloom sandwiched between old newspapers was more than I could risk. A piece of half-folded and half-screwed-up paper lay on the floor. I went to put it in the rubbish bag but checked and unravelled it.

'Valuation of live and dead stock, Dornford Farm, Wootton, 1914' was typed clearly on the front. Inside, all the information about the farm in that year was given. The names of the work horses, their age, colour, and value. The crops and how they had been grown. The machinery, down to the last fork. No, I thought, this is no time for impetuosity and, carefully folding it, put it in the box entitled 'of historic interest'.

In the centre of the room was a huge pile of books. Some were recent paperbacks, once read and then consigned here. Others were much older and were part of the house and its occupants. Religious fervour had gripped the house in late Victorian times and a wealth of bibles, prayer books and solidly bound volumes of religious intent soon filled a tea chest and spilled out into stacks alongside. Several large pieces of furniture came to light, as did family portraits and pieces of silver, often mentioned by my mother, but hidden out of sight here, like some long-lost temple in an equatorial jungle.

Eventually, all was gone. The floor was clear but for one or two discarded photos, a few marbles and a heap of broken walking sticks by the stark water tanks. The room seemed so much bigger and colder. I walked to the window and let myself take in the view. My underlying feeling of desecration melted a little. I knew I had destroyed a time capsule, like breaking virgin ground. But it had to be done, the roof, the plan, the almighty plan. I took breath and left without looking back. It would be different tomorrow.

To the right of the oak staircase and its landing was a smaller room. It had been boarded out as a bedroom in the last century and had been my bedroom in my late teens. It contained no material of any value at all, but a wealth of memory. My old bed still occupied the corner spot. I sat on it and it was twenty years ago.

One of the last Oxfordshire shows was coming up and I had been honoured with the post of steward to the Ayrshire cattle. As an up and coming young farmer, I was also involved in organising the Young Farmers tent. Helping me with this was a girl from Henley, called Chris. The first two days of the show were about cattle judging. My lasting memory is of a fine cow that won the in-calf cow class on the first day, duly calved overnight, and won the in-milk class the next morning. I was certainly a tadpole amongst wise old frogs, but they were very caring frogs to anyone who showed them the respect they thought they were due. The last day of the show had seen an end to the cattle judging and more time in the Young Farmers tent.

Memories became spots of separated, yet distinct images, joined by abstract emotions that somehow seem different with the passing of time. Whether it is maturity, inexperience - call it what you will - or just simple forgetfulness, my thoughts are of great nervousness, a light head and the knowledge that I have little say in what is happening. We had run a quiz, based on old agricultural tools, many of which had been borrowed from a friend near Henley. These were to be returned that night.

As we left the showground, I knew that my feelings for Chris were conflicting with my knowledge that she was engaged, and engaged to a friend. I knew the engagement was failing and yet felt carried along by an invisible thread, which somehow took the weight of this ball and chain called guilt. The night was a turmoil of light and dark, great joy and great disloyalty, yet, as I finally pulled into the gravel drive of Manor Farm in the early hours, I knew I would never be the same.

Love is blind and, as I stumbled to force an entry through the peeling downstairs loo window, I felt totally numb. I was nearly asleep when my mother came into the room.

'Your father and I were a little late in last night, he wonders if you could feed the cattle.' I thought of saying that he was in decidedly sooner than I, but decided not to and, as I rose to dress, I felt as refreshed and young as a spring lamb on a sunny day.

I bounced on the bed and lay back. I felt the joy flooding back that had been with me then, with the guilt long gone. I sprang to my feet and clapped my hands. It was as yesterday, and I was raring to go.

CHAPTER FIFTEEN

The catalogues for the sale arrived at the end of September, complete with general details, individual pedigrees, and the usual amount of printing errors. I phoned Paul, the auctioneer, to give him my opinion.

'I like the photo on the back, but what happened to the one on the front?' Paul was silent, it was a question he had obviously been asking himself. In a catalogue which was well set out, the photograph on the front looked tired and barely in focus.

'I like the one on the back', said Paul, looking for solace.

'Yes, but who looks at the back? The impression is made, the initial impression, at the front.'

I knew it was too late to change. If I had received mine, many others would have received theirs too. I thought of the hours spent going through negatives, taking the printer's advice, 'How will this look in the centre pages?' Now we had a poor front cover on what was otherwise a good catalogue.

Paul was young and relatively inexperienced at selling, though sale preparation and catalogues had long been his forte. I was keen to build up his confidence and diluted every observation of an error with one of praise for some aspect of his efforts.

Some farmers love to point out faults, whether to auctioneers, accountants, solicitors or whomever, as though this redresses the usual state of superiority these professionals have over them. That many of these faults will have occurred because of a mistake by the farmer in the first place is totally ignored by him, as the joy of being in charge for a fleeting moment is utilised to the full. The catalogues had been sent to all the usual breeders of the area and to many beyond. We waited for any response and, as we worked feverishly to clear the yard and make ready for the marquee erection, that feeling of hopeless commitment swept over me.

Chris's brother, David, had brought some lads to help clear the area of debris. Part of it had been used as a machinery park, stemming from the time when no machine was actually scrapped, but carefully put to one side in case a part was needed. That it never was, would never be the right size or could never be found through the mountainous nettles that soon invaded, is an indictment on the follies of human nature.

Kevin, his bright red hair glowing behind the dullness of his goggles, waited, cutting gear in hand, for another metallic object to need his attention. His eyes, even through the perspex, had the glint of a terrier by a rat-infested corn bin.

'Back a little more', David shouted, as I reversed further into dark and rarely-explored territory. A chain was attached, and I inched the tractor forward, taking the strain and then pulling clear.

'What have we here?', as David and I examined this new catch and Kevin hovered hopefully, waiting for David to say 'cut here' and move away.

It was vital at this time to keep my father otherwise occupied. The work rate would drop to virtually zero if he appeared. With every extraction from the jungle would come a recount on the life history of the machine, no inanimate object here but a living part of his working life. History only likes remembering the good times and such were his reminiscences that we all wondered why any machine was ever superseded at all. Many machines were cut up there and then, and some lifted whole and surprisingly complete, loaded onto a fleet of lorries and taken away to fuel the next passage in man's attempt to design a better implement. In the corner of the area stood an old elevator, which had been used to feed sheaves of grain into a thrashing machine in the days before combine harvesters. It had held court in this part of the yard for as long as I can remember, its long, menacing tines pointing skywards from its timber frame.

As it was cut up, the timber showed little sign of rot and brought to mind the ten-year-old front door that we had just had to replace. This door had been carpenter made, preserved, and managed to disintegrate in a quarter of the time that the elevator had stood idle. Beyond it stood another elevator, this one to be pulled by horses behind a wagon and to load loose hay. By its position, it must have been there longer that its bigger counterpart and through it had grown a gnarled elder bush. Rising to over twenty feet, it had assumed more the air of a tree than a bush. The main drive chain of the machine had long come adrift from its cogs and was now an integral part of the trunk of the tree. We attached a tow chain to the machine to pull it clear before we dealt with the tree. As we pulled and the machine came clear, the old drive chain took the full force and we waited for it to snap. Instead, the tree began to tremble, the ground moved ten yards away and with slow, deliberate action, the tree, roots and several tons of soil keeled over and was pulled clear.

The final week before the sale ran amazingly to plan. Several friends arrived to help prepare the sheep, and soon a system was evolved akin to a car production line. Each sheep would be stood on a stand, its face and legs washed, and identity checked, before a necklace bearing its lot number was put in place. The marquee went up on the Thursday in a huge cruciform shape. The main stem was one hundred feet long, and each of the three points of the cross a further fifty feet. That evening, I stood in the bare interior and felt very small. All the penning, the ring and the seating had still to be installed. Bare stones showed through the parched grass and, though we were well to time with our preparations, the weariness, coupled with the underlying pressure, made me lean against a central pole for support. I looked up into the canvas, already beginning to crack and heave with the growing wind.

'What can you tell me, living canvas, what will I know in two days that I don't know now?'

Another voice brought me away from my dreams and my fears. It was Peter, wanting to set up the bar and looking for taps and power points. Reality has a lot going for it. A helicopter flew low over head and, within minutes, a police car drew into the yard. It was the season for acid house parties and the marquee must have looked very suspicious from above. Satisfied, they left, leaving me with thoughts that this expensive marquee could well have had a double use. Just one night of partying before the sale would have covered all my expenses. But then, I might have finished with no marquee at all as well as no friendly neighbours. I walked back to the house, ready for my supper and unsure whether I had been very sensible not to have considered such a party, or very naive.

Friday dawned bright and clear but, with billowing storm clouds soon appearing from the west, the weatherman's prediction about windy weather looked well-founded. This was not a day for major activity. It was one for final preparations, putting polish on the week's work and making sure tomorrow would be as smooth as possible. Most of the work went on inside the marquee, with penning and ring coming together like an almighty jigsaw. The pedigree sheep, which made up the main part of the sale, had been let out and my eyes fell upon a fine ewe, who was grazing happily. She chewed contentedly, as if knowing that whatever happened, tomorrow would surely come and she would be part of it. I felt myself sharing her confidence.

The foreman of the marquee erection team came up behind me with a worried look on his face. With the marquee up and seating finished, most of the gang had returned to base several hours earlier leaving two behind to look after things.

'I have asked for two more men to be sent up', he said quickly. 'They forecast gales for tonight and I don't want to lose the thing.'

Its position, some hundred yards out in the field and to the west of the barn, was certainly exposed and pictures of an open-air sale in force eight winds were not pretty. Despite our tidying, bits of paper, bags and light debris were already being picked up by the wind and tossed in the air until it was caught on a gate or fence or blown over a village rooftop. Inside the marquee was amazing peace, the feverish activity of the tent men had tightened the ropes, sealed the draughts and cut the flapping canvass to a minimum. In the morning, when openings had to be made for sheep and men to enter, problems would arise, but the wind might be gone by then.

Satisfied that all that could be done was being done, I returned to my state of growing numbness. Being busy is a great sedative and now that we were nearly there, I waited for the sense of foreboding to hit me. Two years' work and over a year of planning would rise or fall in a few minutes. All our plans for the future, the new roof and house alterations, were dependant on a successful outcome. I could picture myself back in the bank manager's office, oozing confidently over my costings and estimates.

'What will the sale come to?', I can hear him now, hovering with pen in hand. Then the numbness would take over again, saving me from giving silly answers to unanswerable questions.

A catalogue had been left lazily on a bale in the barn. I picked it up as a stranger might and read the forward. 'The flock was established in

1975 ...' it began. As I read, the past years flicked before me like an old cine film in a darkened room. Breeding pedigree stock is unlike any other farming. Each animal has an identity which demands something from you. It ceases to be a sheep but is an extension of yourself and your ambition. Hopes and dreams rise with success or are dashed by the failure to achieve those dreams. As with all farming, it must be run as a business, yet one of the vital ingredients cannot be itemised with the assets. I felt like someone about to have an operation, or perhaps to give birth, however that feels. The catalogue was not listing sheep, but parts of me and my ambition. Tomorrow would be judgement on that ambition. I remembered the comments of a fellow and much respected breeder upon receiving his catalogue:

'Bob, I don't think you always breed the best sheep but, by god, you can write a catalogue.'

We went out for the evening. Before, I had considered it unfortunate that the annual cricket club dinner should clash with the eve of the sale, but now it had come I was relieved to get away. Mike Norman, a great friend, cricketer, and coach to James, had accepted an invitation to be guest speaker and was due to join us at home for drinks before leaving for the dinner. Needless to say, I was still upstairs changing when he arrived. The telephone had gone mercifully quiet and soon I was able to put thoughts of the sale to the back of my mind. For the first time in weeks, I felt relaxed. Things were now beyond worry and I was almost drunk with relief before the first whisky touched my lips.

The food was only average and the wine unremarkable, but the evening was a great success. As friends of the speaker, Chris and I were put next to Mike. His speech was remarkable for its sincerity. The observations and anecdotes gleaned from a lifetime on the professional cricketing circuit. That he loved his sport was undeniable, that he lived it with strict adherence to technique as well as the natural poetry that must be in every true sportsman, became obvious. As he relived his life, I could only marvel and hope that one day I could look back on my days as a sheep breeder, if not with the same success, at least with equal conviction and sincerity.

Awards were given out for individual and team successes. The junior sides had done particularly well, and the under-thirteen side, for which James had played when home from school, had won several awards. Cricket clubs must be one of the few institutions where men from all walks of life and nearly any age can be equals. The social aspect as important as the playing; the experience of older players willingly given to bring on the young, the future of the club.

I sat back in my chair and dreamt, some say I slept, I hope I did not snore. The warmth, the drink, the literal lull before the storm was invitation enough to drift into the past. In my dream, I was extracting isolated and unconnected parcels of memory and bringing them together on a bright sunny day, with a cool breeze lifting the smell of newly-cut grass. Faces as lazy, smiling flashes; events snatched from the back corner of my mind and fitted irreverently together to form something that seemed right and true. A young boy was walking out to bat, now he was there, the ball struck towards the boundary, the victory run amid cheers. Retired old men smiling, onlookers toasting, senior players congratulating and young boys sharing in the glorious moment. A victory with a sea of faces and among them, larger and happier, the young boy with the victory run, the future.

Whatever romantic notions the evening may have lulled me into, the gale force wind, which nearly knocked us over as we left, soon brought me round. As Chris drove us home, my thoughts were of the marquee. Looking back, I should have been worried, both for the marquee that night and for the practicality of the sale the next day. That we arrived at the marquee with me still in a truly happy and confident mood is probably more a reflection on the mix of tiredness and alcohol than of anything else.

At three in the morning, the tent men were all hard at work, driving in pegs, tightening ropes and lashing canvass. At least they're not on a sailing ship with tossing waves ready to pluck them from their perches, I thought, my mind still anxious not to take in the reality of the situation. We slipped inside.

There was an eery feel, almost a vacuum where you could hear your heartbeat in the internal stillness, yet listen to the roar of the gale outside. It was snug and warm. So long as people had the confidence to travel, they would certainly be comfortable in here. The marquee had been expensive, an extra bid per sheep I had calculated. Well, I would certainly be comfortable enough to stay in here rather than face the anger that was outside. Comfortable enough to bid again and again? I left the question unanswered.

To Chris's amazement I slept like a log, the evening had given me that too! I woke feeling refreshed and relaxed. Any worries of a thick head soon went, as I slid from the bed and peered through the curtains. The winds were still rough, but no worse than last night. The worst must be passed, I told myself, and dressed.

Robin, the Galloway farmer's son who had been down for the two previous years to help with the lambing, had done us the honour of coming back for the sale and had brought his attractive girlfriend and future wife, Fiona. They had both joined us in the barn as the first light threatened to find its way through the fleeting clouds. We had the job of sorting the sheep, which had been loose housed in the big barn overnight, and running them over to the sale marquee. There they would be penned in small groups in catalogue order. Sheep hate moving in the dark but, with good planning and ample handlers, we were making good progress. It was only a matter of time, of course, before one bunch broke the wrong way and seemed destined to escape up a side alley. Robin is known for his dog, of which he is justly proud. However, on this occasion, Ben was still in Scotland. Robin had mentioned several times how much easier it would have been with his well-trained Scottish dog instead of these cumbersome Englishmen. My father couldn't resist shouting out,

'Robin, where's your dog?' Before he could answer, Fiona appeared through an opening and headed off the sheep.

'Here she is!'

We all fell about laughing.

With the tension broken and the sheep penned, we returned to the house for a well-earned breakfast. The light was growing now and made the wind seem lighter. Paul arrived, having lain awake most of the night, picturing flying marquees and scenes of chaos and destruction. He found our relaxed state bewildering and soon left to put up the 'To the sale' signs on the main access roads. Some friends who had travelled long distances came in for breakfast. The main entrance to the sale was through the farmyard and not past the house. It was not until I reached the far side of the big barn that I saw a good show of cars and trailers, lorries and vans of every shape and size. My worst fears that few would leave home seemed unfounded. Our next job was to persuade them to bid.

The last hour before the sale commenced was the worst. Breeders stepping from pen to pen, consulting fathers or sons, writing in catalogues, checking sheep, expressionless with concentration, giving nothing away. The plan for getting sheep to the ring and away again was double-checked, the group of helpers ready to give the sheep a final wipe before they entered.

Nathan, looking lean, potentially angry and always in need of another meal, hovered with cloth in hand. He had only been with us for a week but already his gritty Lancashire wit had emerged as he had shown how he could work. The job of preparing the sheep for sale had been an ongoing determination of making the next sheep look better than the last.

'This leg needs a little more scrubbing', as he had set to with a bent back and powerful arm. The need not to trim any wayward wool on the pedigree ewes he found very frustrating.

'Just a bit off here and a tidy round the neck', he would say, 'no one will ever know.' My denial of this request was met with painful bewilderment.

'It's like sending a daughter to a ball only half ready, it's not right!'

He finally accepted my ruling, though he never really understood or agreed with it. At last, we came to the few cross-bred ewes, which were to be sold at the end of the sale.

'These aren't pedigree, that clipping law doesn't apply, does it?' He bounced, I smiled.

'No, Nathan, it doesn't apply.' He bounded over to his box and emerged with his hand shears.

'If I just tidy them around the head, they will look a lot better, much more level.' He was as a boy in a sweet shop, at last he felt he was doing a proper job.

'Have you got a minute to discuss prices', the auctioneer whispered in my ear.

He opened the catalogue and ran his finger down the page. The lot numbers stood out in bold print, three to a page. Alongside each, the identity of the sheep and, below, its parents through to its grandparents, with notes to highlight any factors of special importance - a book of family trees. As individuals met my gaze, their own unique number brought up pictures in my mind. Joyful moments of sheep I had known, some I missed and wanted to retrieve. Others I was happy to let go. Yet now was not a time for romance, but for cold economics. The auctioneer looked at me, as though I was overcome by nerves or lost to worry.

'Yes, certainly, we must know where we stand. If we can get the first of each category sorted out, the rest should follow on.' I tried to sound cold and calculating. He agreed and made some notes. I looked at him and thought 'yes, these are just sheep to you'. I knew they could be nothing more.

We sat in his car, writing in minimum prices, under which we would not sell. The idea of not selling had not been an option I had wanted to consider, but it must be done and so, with figures based on recent national sales, we fixed a minimum value for each sheep.

The ring was raised some eighteen inches above the ground and was about six feet square. I climbed into the ring as the first sheep entered and the auctioneer lurched into his introductory spiel. The first five sheep were older ewes, put in to start the sale and offering some daughters of Panzer, the English National Champion three years before. They sold increasingly well, and I was afraid that it was only the Panzer daughters that would be wanted.

The first yearling ewe entered the ring, a strong sheep with good breed points. Already the ring was slippery, and I moved her round slowly, using my crook to present her. The ring was surrounded by an ever-increasing company. Many I knew, many were just friends that had come to give moral support. Some were strangers with the nervous look of potential bidders, others sat and ate or drank. No indication of the trade could be gleaned, as the air of expectancy hung heavily and the wind still roared outside, a million miles away.

The first bid was two hundred guineas, about half my value and at three hundred it seemed to stick. The sheep stood in the centre of the ring and looked proudly about her. The auctioneer was working hard, striving for reaction from buyers not wanting to make the first move.

'Have we any more for this fine sheep?', he demanded, but all eyes were on the sheep.

She stood still, moving only her head in short irate snatches and her ears in sharp backward and forward movements, as a radar striving to pick up more than just the sound, but the feeling and atmosphere too. She was the first to sense the change. A thick-set gentleman in the middle row bid first, prompting a lady at the back. The bidding rose in fifty and then hundred-guinea bids, as an old engine picking up steam. I dimly remember hearing a thousand mentioned and thinking I must not smile or look happy. I must muster the 'you are nearly at its value' look and be reassuring. At fourteen hundred guineas it was knocked down to a new breeder from the north.

The die had been cast and the day progressed as I could not have dreamt. Like a groom at a wedding, I could only see glimpses through my haze of excitement. The hectic scene of trailers, of comings and goings, of people talking, asking, congratulating. I went outside for some air and hardly noticed that the wind had gone and the sun was trying to show its fleeting face before dusk took over.

I entered the barn where we had prepared the sheep and housed them the previous night. It now stood huge and empty. The catalogue still lay open on the bale where I had left it a lifetime ago. I sat down and picked it up. It was no longer a plan of action, a commitment, a hope, but a marker of what had gone, a piece of history. As I thumbed through its soiled pages, glimpses returned, some I could not remember seeing before.

'Sold to the gentleman in the front row', roared the auctioneer triumphantly, as a young granddaughter of 'granny', one of the foundation ewes I had bought privately in Scotland in the early days, found the open gate and ran from the sale ring.

I waited for the next sheep to enter. A leggy, nervous sheep was finally pushed forward. She stood with her head down and looked at the floor. I moved towards her.

'I didn't like you when you were born, I haven't liked you since, and I'm sure I don't like you now', I whispered under my breath. 'How the hell are we going to sell you?' Beneath the auctioneer's confidence I could sense that he, too, could sense problems.

A bid from the same gentleman in the front row broke the ice, in steady stages it crept higher... 'and it's still a very cheap sheep, let them look at her, Bob', urged the auctioneer. She looked at me, a hint of pride, of defiance, of a rebellious daughter who has never been understood. As she left the ring at a very good price, I felt strangely empty. I didn't feel great loss, just emptiness at losing something I had never really known.

'There's a brew in the house, Bob.' A friend's voice nervously broke my distant soul search. I suddenly felt stiff and very cold. I returned to the house, where already friends, old and new, were eating and drinking. I sat down and took a breath. Chris brought me a cup of tea and smiled. I sipped my tea and smiled too. The auctioneer approached with the broadest of grins, passing me a catalogue containing all the prices.

'I've calculated the averages, I doubt it will be beaten this year', and he happily accepted a glass of bubbles to celebrate.

The next morning, the elation of the previous day was quiet and subdued. It must have settled some hours before I woke and, mixed with the realisation that I was very tired, taken on a purely mental mode. To move even a finger seemed a mighty effort. I drifted back into a wonderful semi-sleep and tried to listen for the wind. It gave no sound and the well-risen sun had few challengers in its sky today.

The roofers had arrived a week before and started on the back of the house, where they would give least disturbance before the sale, stripping off the old Stonefield slates and sliding them carefully to the ground below. The oak battens glistened white and damp. The main timbers were in good order, we had caught them just in time and, with the weather now set fair, progress was rapid. The reassuring dullness of new felt against the new brown battens took away the hollowness of a house without a roof. The sound of nails echoing from above brought the distant thoughts to reality. I sat up and got up in one movement, scared that temptation might draw me back to that warm, inviting pillow.

Several friends had stayed overnight and were already up, clearing the debris of the night before. I commented on my good timing as the hoover ran over the last bit of carpet and the sound of bacon crackled from the kitchen. Many sheep had been left for collection today and already nervous couples, waving crumpled sales notes, were coming to the door. For the next week, I drifted between relief and illusion, only touching reality on rare occasions. I knew the world was going on around me, the sound of the roof, the patch where the marquee had been, the deserted barn and bags and bags of litter. The main flock was away on pasture and, when the last sold sheep had been collected, a mock empty peace descended.

Harry, that extrovert Harry, called in during the week after the sale. Many friends called that week with congratulations, describing the event as they had seen it. Often, they were friends I had not seen, or even known were there; sometimes they were old and respected ones whose presence had been a great settler on the day. One of these was John Smith.

My paternal grandfather had come down from Scotland in the twenties to manage a farm for his father and our families had been close ever since. My maternal grandfather had been a much-respected breeder of dairy shorthorn cattle and a great friend and neighbour of the Smiths. In areas such as this, where farming families went on for generations, a family-like bond of respect develops, which can supersede everyday events. I remembered my father and John sitting in a front row at the sale, looking like two mischievous schoolboys. They were looking about them, talking and often laughing. Concentrating, not as lawyers might, but as two who want to absorb an atmosphere and miss nothing.

'What would your grandfather have made of this sale?', he had said, as he shook my hand before sipping a whisky from a large, cut-glass tumbler, which looked small compared with his John Bull character and appearance.

'They should have been cows, of course, but I think he would have forgiven you for that.' I think he was right. It is strange that, however one thinks positively about the future, one always looks back apologetically for support. I can remember thinking of my grandfather before the sale, of hoping I would live up to the standards that he had set.

It had been thirty years almost to the month that the dairy herd had been sold, in a marquee and in this very field. I can remember as a small boy, running around, getting in the way, playing tig with the cowman's son. What had changed, what had I achieved? Sheep had replaced cattle, as they would have been many years before; and most of the crops of barley, vetches and sainfoin could have been seen here a hundred years ago.

In a drawer in the big Sitting Room is a catalogue of the farm sale, when my great-grandfather had ceased to be tenant and had bought the farm. Agriculturally, little had changed, yet in the two years since we had started Bed and Breakfast, developed the sheep flock, and created the lake, we had become a farm of today rather than yesterday. It is easy to feel angry, to feel that people do not understand farmers or farming, their history, traditions, and in-born responsibilities. They do not want to know, only criticise, moralise and have their say. But farms today must be of the people and for the people, as is this small, basic farm, with big house and dry land, the valley an ever-present oasis.

I left the house and walked along the tall hedge that ran away from the buildings. Its margins were strewn with the debris of the night. Out across the field, the leaves of autumn; nearer, the small branches and twigs; on the headland itself, larger boughs bent over in the storm, never to return. Initially a site of devastation, of loss, but, as the morning breeze brought the clear sky and flashing sun, the view became one of deviance. A covey of partridge rose and disappeared over the hedge disturbing a solitary ewe. Deemed too lame to be sold, she had been put out to graze and already showed barely a sign of lameness.

Harry was still in the kitchen, persuading Chris that she really could do Christmas lunch for seventy this year; his Vintage Austin Club would not be the same without. As I left, four Bed and Breakfast guests arrived. I showed them in and continued to feed the sheep. Winter came, as it does, and Christmas before we were ready. The new year brought the real winter and one February morning I woke with a start. It was snowing and I looked at the clock: 4:27. I got up and went downstairs, lit the fire and made some tea. I stood by the window and cradled my cup. Flurries wafted past the streetlight on the corner and settled on the garden wall. In many ways it could have been two years before, the wagon on the wall, the tall carved cupboard, the copper above the fire, yet the chill of the world had gone.

Tomorrow was a new day and I looked forward to it.

Lightning Source UK Ltd.
Milton Keynes UK
UKHW010746061120
372867UK00006B/263